LATINA CHRISTIANA

An Introduction to Christian Latin

— BOOK II —

STUDENT BOOK

By Cheryl Lowe

CLASSICAL TRIVIUM CORE SERIES

LATINA CHRISTIANA: STUDENT BOOK II

Third Edition © 2002 Memoria Press
ISBN #: 1-930953-07-0

First Edition 1998, Second Edition 2000
The third edition student book may be used with the
the second edition teacher manual.

4103 Bishop Lane, Louisville, KY 40218
www.memoriapress.com

Table of **Contents**

LESSONS

APPENDICES

Vocabulary

1st Conjugation Verbs

amo	clamo	occupo
porto	voco	appello
laudo	supero	narro
oro	adoro	do
laboro	libero	habito
navigo	ambulo	lavo
paro	pugno	
specto	judico	

2nd Conjugation Verbs

moneo	doceo
video	debeo
terreo	prohibeo
habeo	jubeo
moveo	sedeo
timeo	

Grammar Forms

Verb endings

S.	Pl.

1st Conjugation

S.	Pl.

2nd Conjugation

S.	Pl.

Present tense

S.	Pl.	1st S.	1st Pl.	2nd S.	2nd Pl.
o	mus	porto	portamus	moneo	monemus
s	tis	portas	portatis	mones	monetis
t	nt	portat	portant	monet	monent

Future tense

S.	Pl.	1st S.	1st Pl.	2nd S.	2nd Pl.
bo	bimus	portabo	portabimus	monebo	monebimus
bis	bitis	portabis	portabitis	monebis	monebitis
bit	bunt	portabit	portabunt	monebit	monebunt

Imperfect tense

S.	Pl.	1st S.	1st Pl.	2nd S.	2nd Pl.
bam	bamus	portabam	portabamus	monebam	monebamus
bas	batis	portabas	portabatis	monebas	monebatis
bat	bant	portabat	portabant	monebat	monebant

Present Tense Irregular verbs

sum	sumus
es	estis
est	sunt
pos-sum	pos-sumus
pot-es	pot-estis
pot-est	pos-sunt

Latin Sayings

Ora et Labora
Mater Italiae - Roma
Caelum et Terra
E pluribus unum
Labor omnia vincit
mea culpa
Anno Domini, A.D.

A. Give the three English translations for each verb.

1. portat _gate, enterance, doorway_
2. laudo _praise, to give praise_
3. docetis _you taught, you learned, you [aquired] skill_
4. videmus _we saw, we observed, we understand_

B. Complete these sentences by adding "t" or "nt" to the verb. Translate three ways.

1. Puellae ora_t_ . _____
   _____
   _____

2. Servus ora_nt_ . _____
   _____
   _____

3. Nauta voca_t_ . _____
   _____
   _____

4. Nautae voca_t_ . _____
   _____
   _____

5. Servi sede_nt_ . _____
   _____
   _____

6. Amicus sede_nt_ . _____
   _____
   _____

7. Regnum supera_t_ . _____
   _____
   _____

8. Regna supera_nt_ . _____
   _____
   _____

C. Circle the tense ending and translate.

1. lauda**bant** _they praised_
2. amabimus _we will love_
3. habitabatis) _____
4. mon**ent** _they advise_
5. doce**bat** _(he, she, it) teached_
6. porta**bunt** _~~they entered, they gated~~ they will enter_
7. vide**bis** _you will see; you will watch; you will observe._
8. jube**bas** _____
9. judica**bam** _____
10. habe**batis** _____

D. Translate.

1. I am fighting. _____

2. They are preventing. _____

3. She does wash. _____

4. They are not shouting. _____

5. You do judge. _____

6. You (pl.) are giving. _____

7. They do shout. _____

8. He is walking. _____

9. They move. _____

10. We do pray. _____

E. Conjugate in the present, imperfect and future.

1.

present		
do	domas
dos	dotis
dot	dont

imperfect		
dobo	dobimus
dobis	dobitis
dobit	dobunt

future		
dobam	dobamus
dobas	dobatis
dobat	dobant

2.

jubeo	jubemus
jubes	jubetis
jubet	jubent

jubebo	jubebimus
jubebis	jubebitis
jubebit	jubebunt

jubebam	jubebamus
jubebas	jubebatis
jubebat	jubebant

F. Use each derivative in a sentence.

1. amateur _____

2. vocal _____

3. laudable _____

4. ambulance _____

5. laboratory _____

6. narrator _____

7. spectator _____

8. timid _____

Vocabulary

Roma, ae	mensa
Italia, ae	toga
gloria	patria
vita	culpa
aqua	Maria
memoria	fuga
victoria	luna

terra	unda
lingua	Hispania
via	silva
fortuna	stella
herba	ursa
nauta	ira
Gallia	gratia
femina	hora
filia	pecunia

regina	ecclesia
puella	aquila
corona	aurora
mora	auriga
insula	pugna
injuria	fenestra
cena	fama

Grammar Forms
Case Endings

	S.	*Pl.*
nominative	a	ae
genitive	ae	arum
dative	ae	is
accusative	am	as
ablative	a	is

Noun Forms

	S.	*Pl.*
nominative	mens-a	mens-ae
genitive	mens-ae	mens-arum
dative	mens-ae	mens-is
accusative	mens-am	mens-as
ablative	mens-a	mens-is

Pronoun Forms
First person

S.	*Pl.*
ego	nos
mei	nostri, nostrum
mihi	nobis
me	nos
me	nobis

Second person

S.	*Pl.*
tu	vos
tui	vestri, vestrum
tibi	vobis
te	vos
te	vobis

Latin Sayings

> Semper Fidelis
>
> Senatus Populusque Romanus, S.P.Q.R.
>
> stupor mundi
>
> ante bellum
>
> Excelsior
>
> Sanctus, Sanctus, Sanctus, Dominus Deus Sabaoth

Grammar

1. List all five Latin cases. _____

   _____

   _____

   _____

   _____

2. A word that receives the action of a verb is a _____.

3. The direct object is always in the _____ case.

4. Fill in these boxes with the normal word order of a Latin sentence.

   [   ]   [   ]   [   ]

Drill A. Write these nouns in the accusative singular and plural.

1. cena _____   3. herba _____

   _____   _____

2. hora _____   4. toga _____

   _____   _____

Drill B. Identify the case and number of these noun forms. For some words there will be more than one answer.

1. viam _____

2. pecuniae _____

3. memoriis _____

4. fugarum _____

5. culpa _____

Exercise A. Underline the direct object and translate.

Translate verbs three ways. (except # 4)

1. Puella cenam parat. _____

    _____ _____ _____

2. Roma insulas occupat. _____

    _____ _____ _____

3. Maria fenestras lavat. _____

    _____ _____ _____

4. Femina aquam portabit. _____

5. Filia stellas videt. _____

    _____ _____ _____

Exercise B. Underline direct object and translate into Latin.

1. We are preparing dinner. _____

2. The girls are moving the tables. _____

3. The Queen has a crown. _____

4. The waves frighten the girls. _____

Derivatives. Use each derivative in a sentence.

1. lunar _____

2. stellar _____

3. peninsula _____

4. glorious _____

5. coronation _____

Vocabulary

Masculine	Neuter
servus, i	bellum, i
amicus, i	donum, i
annus	oppidum
filius	telum
dominus	verbum
Deus	regnum
Christus	frumentum
legatus	signum
discipulus	imperium
gladius	proelium
murus	gaudium
populus	auxilium
animus	debitum
mundus	caelum
socius	peccatum
nuntius	vallum
barbarus	praemium
campus	vinum
capillus	tergum
cibus	forum
equus	
ventus	
locus	
agnus	
oculus	
hortus	
nimbus	
ludus	

Grammar Forms

Masculine
Case endings

S.	Pl.
us	i
i	orum
o	is
um	os
o	is

Noun Forms

serv-us	serv-i
serv-i	serv-orum
serv-o	serv-is
serv-um	serv-os
serv-o	serv-is

Neuter
Case Endings

um	a
i	orum
o	is
um	a
o	is

Noun Forms

don-um	don-a
don-i	don-orum
don-o	don-is
don-um	don-a
don-o	don-is

Latin Sayings

> Novus ordo seclorum
>
> Nunc aut numquam
>
> Veni, vidi, vici
>
> Agnus Dei, qui tollis peccata mundi.
>
> Rident stolidi verba Latina
>
> Quo vadis

Grammar

1. A word that *receives* the action of a verb is a _____ and is put in the _____ case.

2. The person or thing that *performs* the action of the verb is the _____ and is put in the _____ case.

3. The genitive singular of first declension nouns is _____ and of second declension nouns is _____.

Drill A. Give the accusative singular and plural of these second declension masculine nouns.

1. capillus   _____   _____

2. oculus   _____   _____

3. nimbus   _____   _____

4. campus   _____   _____

Drill B. Identify the case and number of these noun forms. For some words there will be more than one answer.

1. vento   _____

2. sociis   _____

3. amicorum   _____

4. equi   _____

5. agnum   _____

Exercise A. Underline the direct object and translate.
For 1 & 2 translate verbs three ways.

1. Deus mundum amat.

   _____

   _____   _____   _____

2. Roma barbaros superat.

   _____

   _____   _____   _____

3. Legatus gladium portat.

   _____

4. Christus discipulos habet.

   _____

5. Amicus hortum spectabat.

   _____

Exercise B. Underline direct object and translate into Latin.

1. The town has an ally.

   _____

2. The master frees the slaves.

   _____

3. The lieutenant sees the horses.

   _____

4. The people fear the Lord.

   _____

5. The son sees the winds and the clouds.

   _____

Derivatives. Use each derivative in a sentence.

1. social _____

2. donate _____

3. discipline _____

4. annual _____

5. mural _____

Vocabulary

3rd Declension

frater, fratris
pater, patris
mater, matris
centurio, centurionis
civitas, civitatis
soror, sororis
veritas, veritatis
Caesar, Caesaris
dolor, doloris
imperator, imperatoris
caput, capitis, *n.*
hostis, hostis, *c.*
ordo, ordinis, *m.*
tempus, temporis
virtus, virtutis
miles, militis
flumen, fluminis, *n.*
legio, legionis, *f.*
canis, canis, *c.*

nomen, nominis, *n.*
lux, lucis, *f.*
rex, regis
lex, legis, *f.*
urbs, urbis, *f.*
vox, vocis, *f.*
homo, hominis
pax, pacis, *f.*
ignis, ignis. *f.*
collis, collis, *m.*
navis, navis, *f.*
nox, noctis, *f.*
crux, crucis, *f.*
pons, pontis, *m.*
gens, gentis, *f.*
pars, partis, *f.*
mons, montis, *m.*
mors, mortis, *f.*
corpus, corporis

Constellations

virgo
libra
scorpio
sagittarius
capricorn
aquarius
pisces
aries
taurus
geminus
cancer
leo

Numbers

unus	quinque	novem
duo	sex	decem
tres	septem	centum
quattuor	octo	mille

Latin Sayings

Alma mater
Pax Romana
Miles Christi sum
Vox Populi, Vox Dei
Signum crucis
Et tu Brute?

Grammar. **Give the nominative and genitive** *singular* **endings for each declension.**

1.　　　　First Declension　　　Second Declension　　　Third Declension

nominative _____　　_____　　_____

genitive _____　　_____　　_____

2. What case is used to (a) identify the declension? _____

　(b) find the stem? _____　Why? _____

Drill A. Give the genitive singular for each Third Declension noun. Translate.

1. dolor　　_____　_____

2. mors　　_____　_____

3. civitas　　_____　_____

4. miles　　_____　_____

5. homo　　_____　_____

6. caput　　_____　_____

7. nomen　　_____　_____

8. flumen　　_____　_____

9. nox　　_____　_____

Drill B. Give the acc. sing. and pl. of these 2nd decl. neuter nouns from Lesson III.

1. tergum　_____ _____　3. auxilium　_____ _____

2. proelium　_____ _____　4. praemium　_____ _____

Drill C. Give the case and number of these noun forms. For some there will be more than one answer. Nouns are from Lesson III.

1. gaudio   _____ _____

2. fora   _____ _____

3. debitorum   _____ _____

4. belli   _____ _____

5. caelis   _____ _____

Exercise A. Underline the direct object and translate.

1. Miles tela parabat.   _____

2. Dominus praemia dat.   _____

3. Roma oppida occupat.   _____

4. Navis frumentum portat   _____

Exercise B. Translate into Latin.

1. Mother does not like wars. (Use *amo* for like) _____

2. Caesar likes battles. _____

3. The city has a rampart. _____

4. The emperor is giving a gift. _____

Derivatives. Use each derivative in a sentence.

1. virtue _____

2. regal _____

3. legislature _____

4. nocturnal _____

5. patriarch _____

_____

Vocabulary

Adjectives

altus, a, um
bonus, a, um
longus
malus
multus
magnus
plenus
sanctus
tutus
parvus
aeternus
certus
primus
secundus
tertius
proximus
summus
totus
solus
novus
tuus
meus

Adverbs

semper
saepe
nunc
clam
non
bene
numquam

Prepositions

ante
post
inter
contra
sub
supra
ex

Other Words

Jesus
sicut
et

Grammar Forms

First and Second Declension Adjectives

Masc.	Fem.	Neut.
	Singular	
bon-us	bon-a	bon-um
bon-i	bon-ae	bon-i
bon-o	bon-ae	bon-o
bon-um	bon-am	bon-um
bon-o	bon-a	bon-o
	Plural	
bon-i	bon-ae	bon-a
bon-orum	bon-arum	bon-orum
bon-is	bon-is	bon-is
bon-os	bon-as	bon-a
bon-is	bon-is	bon-is

Grammar

1. Define *adjective*. _____ .

2. Adjectives agree with their nouns in _____ , _____ , and

   _____ .

3. The three genders of nouns in Latin are _____ , _____ ,

   and _____ .

Exercise A. Underline the direct object and its adjective. Translate.

1. Regina parvum filium amat. _____

   _____

2. Frater multum cibum habet. _____

   _____

3. Barbari multos capillos habent. _____

   _____

4. Rex proxima oppida occupabat. _____

   _____

5. Puellae filium meum laudabunt. _____

   _____

Exercise B. Underline the subject and its adjective. Translate.

1. Filius meus filiam tuam amat. _____

   _____

2. Servus malus equos terrebat. _____

   _____

3. Legatus novus puellas vocabit. _____

   _____

4. Magnae feminae longas mensas movent. _____

   _____

5. Sanctus Deus peccata non amat. _____

   _____

Exercise C. Translate into Latin.

1. Your daughter adores horses.   _____

    _____

2. He will see the high wall.   _____

    _____

3. Rome loves great glory.   _____

    _____

4. God gives eternal life.   _____

    _____

Derivatives. Use a derivative from today's lesson.

1. A large number of people or things is a _____.

2. An answer that is close but not exact is _____.

3. _____ means to make holy.

4. Gorillas like _____ of bananas.

REVIEW ALL VOCABULARY FROM LESSONS I-V

Drill A. Mark the correct case or cases and number. Translate.

	Nom.	Acc.	S.	Pl.	Meaning
1. loci	_____	_____	___ ___	_____
2. gaudium	_____	_____	___ ___	_____
3. barbarum	_____	_____	___ ___	_____
4. peccata	_____	_____	___ ___	_____
5. fama	_____	_____	___ ___	_____
6. tergum	_____	_____	___ ___	_____
7. muros	_____	_____	___ ___	_____
8. hortum	_____	_____	___ ___	_____
9. debita	_____	_____	___ ___	_____
10. fuga	_____	_____	___ ___	_____
11. morae	_____	_____	___ ___	_____
12. auxilium	_____	_____	___ ___	_____

READING # 1
Jesus Christus

Jesus est homo. Jesus est Deus. Jesus et homo et[1] Deus est. Jesus puellas et feminas et pueros et homines[2] amat. Jesus servos et nautas et discipulos amat. Jesus in[3] mundum venit[4]. Jesus in terra ambulabat. Jesus multas fabulas narrabat. Jesus in aqua ambulabat. Jesus mundum superabat. Jesus nunc est in Caelo[5]. Jesus est Christus.

---

[1] et...et,   both... and
[2] acc. pl. of homo
[3] into (in subsequent sentences in means *in* or *on*)
[4] came
[5] Heaven

LESSON VI

Vocabulary

1.	umbra, ae	*shadow*
2.	tuba, ae	*trumpet*
3.	Lucia, ae	*Lucy*
4.	porta, ae	*gate, door*
5.	villa, ae	*farmhouse*
6.	fabula, ae	*story*
7.	provincia, ae	*province*
8.	sella, ae	*chair*

Latin Saying

Retro Satana!

Get thee behind me, Satan!

Grammar

First Declension

Singular

	Form	Meaning	Use
Nominative	**mens-a**	the (a) table	subject, predicate noun
Genitive	**mens-ae**	of the table	possessive, *of* phrases
Dative	**mens-ae**	to/for the table	indirect object
Accusative	**mens-am**	the (a) table	direct object
Ablative	**mens-a**	by/with/from the table	prepositional objects

Plural

	Form	Meaning	Use
Nom.	**mens-ae**	the tables	subject, predicate noun
Gen.	**mens-arum**	of the tables	possessive, *of* phrases
Dat.	**mens-is**	to/for the tables	indirect object
Acc.	**mens-as**	the tables	direct object
Abl.	**mens-is**	by/with/from the tables	prepositional objects

Grammar

1. The ablative case is the _____ case.

2. The dative case is the _____ case.

Drill A. Identify case and number. Translate using meanings from table.

Some words will have more than one answer.

1. umbrarum _____ _____ _____

2. villam _____ _____ _____

3. sellas _____ _____ _____

4. portis _____ _____ _____

5. fabulas _____ _____ _____

6. Lucia _____ _____ _____

7. provinciae _____ _____ _____

8. tubis _____ _____ _____

9. umbras _____ _____ _____

Drill B. Verb review. Translate.

1. We will fear. _____

2. They were commanding. _____

3. You (s.) do work. _____

4. You (pl.) owe. _____

5. I will overcome. _____

6. He is adoring. _____

7. We were fighting. _____

8. They will live. _____

Exercise A. Translate sentences with <u>adjectives modifying subjects.</u>

1. <u>Lucia bona</u> fabulas narrabit. _____

2. <u>Memoriae bonae</u> gaudium dant. _____

3. <u>Amicus meus</u> aquilam videt. _____

4. <u>Parva puella</u> equum vocabat. _____

5. <u>Miles malus</u> villam occupat. _____

Exercise B. Translate into Latin. Remember the usual word order of a Latin sentence.

1. Lucy was moving the chairs. _____

2. Rome was seizing the province. _____

3. The girls will carry the trumpets. _____

4. Lucy sees the shadow. _____

5. The farmhouse has new gates. _____

Derivatives. Use each derivative in a sentence.

1. fabulous _____

2. umbrella _____

3. portal _____

4. province _____

LESSON VII

Vocabulary

Latin Saying

Natura non facit saltum

*Nature does not
 make leaps*

1.	scientia, ae	*knowledge*
2.	ara, ae	*altar*
3.	casa, ae	*cottage*
4.	cithara, ae	*harp*
5.	taberna, ae	*shop*
6.	natura, ae	*nature*
7.	janua, ae	*door, entrance*
8.	epistula, ae	*letter*
9.	tabella, ae	*tablet*
10.	culina, ae	*kitchen*
11.	agricola, ae, *m.*	*farmer*
12.	poeta, ae, *m.*	*poet*

Grammar

1. The stem of a Latin noun is always found by dropping the ending from the

   _____.

2. All nouns whose genitive singular ends in **ae** belong to the _____

   declension.

3. Three first-declension nouns that are masculine are _____, _____,

   and _____.

Drill A. Identify case and number. Translate using meanings from table.
Some words will have more than one answer.

1. tabernae _____ _____

2. epistularum _____ _____

3. januas _____ _____

4. citharis _____ _____

5. culinarum _____ _____

6. poetis _____ _____

7. ara _____ _____

8. scientiam _____ _____

Drill B. Decline.

1. _____janua nova_____ _____ 2. _____poeta bonus_____ _____

   _____ _____ _____ _____

   _____ _____ _____ _____

   _____ _____ _____ _____

Exercise A. Translate these sentences with <u>adjectives modifying direct objects</u>.

1. Roma <u>multas terras</u> superabit. _____

   _____

2. Imperator <u>multa oppida</u> superabat. _____

   _____

3. Populus <u>longa bella</u> non amat. _____

   _____

4. Mater <u>dona nova</u> adorabit. _____

   _____

Exercise B. Underline the direct object and its adjective if there is one. Translate.

1. The student carries a small tablet. _____

2. The students carry large tablets. _____

3. The kitchen has a table and chair. _____

4. The poet loves the harp. _____

5. The farmer sees the shop. _____

Derivatives. Complete sentences with derivatives from today's lesson.

1. _____ means having to do with cooking and eating.

2. If you violate your _____ you will become hardened to sin.

3. _____ is the cultivation of the land.

4. _____ means mentally awake and aware.

LESSON VIII

Vocabulary

1.	ager, agri	*field*
2.	liber, libri	*book*
3.	magister, magistri	*master, teacher*
4.	Gallus, i	*a Gaul*
5.	Romanus, i	*a Roman*
6.	vicus, i	*town, village*
7.	apostolus, i	*apostle*
8.	Christianus, i	*a Christian*
9.	lupus, i	*wolf*
10.	Marcus, i	*Mark*

Latin Saying

Magister dixit

The master has spoken

Grammar Forms

Second Declension nouns ending in *er*

S.	Pl.
ager	agr-i
agr-i	agr-orum
agr-o	agr-is
agr-um	agr-os
agr-o	agr-is

Sayings. Translate.

1. Retro Satana! _____

2. Natura non facit saltum. _____

3. Tibi gratias ago. _____

Drill A. Identify case and number. Translate using meanings from table.
Some words will have more than one answer.

1. vico _____ _____ _____

2. apostoli _____ _____ _____

3. Romanorum _____ _____ _____

4. Christianos _____ _____ _____

5. libris _____ _____ _____

6. lupum _____ _____ _____

Drill B. Give the following forms.

1. *genitive singular*: sella, vicus _____ _____

2. *accusative plural*: villa, lupus _____ _____

3. *dative plural*: vita, agnus _____ _____

Drill C. Decline.

1. _____liber_____ _____ 2. _____magister_____ _____

_____ _____   _____ _____

_____ _____   _____ _____

_____ _____   _____ _____

_____ _____   _____ _____

Exercise A. Translate.

1. Lucia librum habet. _____

2. Romani Gallos superant. _____

3. Agricola lupum non amat. _____

4. Christiani Deum laudant. _____

5. Christus apostolos vocabat. _____

Exercise B. Translate.

1. The lamb does not love the wolf. _____

2. The teacher was waiting for the students. _____

3. The Gauls will seize the village. _____

4. The books are new. _____

Derivatives. Give English derivatives for the first three words in today's lesson. From what form of the Latin word do the English derivatives come?

_____

_____

_____

LESSON IX

Vocabulary

1.	periculum, i	*danger, peril*
2.	scutum, i	*shield*
3.	studium, i	*enthusiasm, zeal, learning*
4.	saeculum, i	*time, period, age, world*
5.	Evangelium, i	*Gospel*
6.	mandatum, i	*command, commandment*
7.	principium, i	*beginning, foundation*
8.	angelus, i	*angel*
9.	puer, pueri	*boy*
10.	vir, viri	*man, husband*

Latin Saying

Repetitio mater studiorum

Repetition is the mother of learning

Grammar Forms

Second Declension nouns ending in *er, ir*

S.	Pl.
puer	puer-i
puer-i	puer-orum
puer-o	puer-is
puer-um	puer-os
puer-o	puer-is

Sayings. Translate.

1. The master has spoken. _____

2. Nature does not make leaps. _____

3. Get thee behind me, Satan! _____

4. Sicut erat in principio et nunc et semper et in saecula saeculorum.

   _____

5. Novus ordo seclorum. _____

Drill A. Identify case and number. Translate using meanings from table.
Some words will have more than one answer.

1. pericula _____ _____

2. angelorum _____ _____

3. principio _____ _____

4. saeculum _____ _____

5. studio _____ _____

6. scuti _____ _____

Drill B. Give the following forms.

1. *genitive singular*: periculum, angelus, casa

   _____ _____ _____

2. *dative singular*: scientia, Gallus, scutum

   _____ _____ _____

3. *ablative plural*: peccatum, vir, janua

   _____ _____ _____

4. *nominative plural*: agricola, mandatum, puer

   _____ _____ _____

EXERCISES *for Lesson IX*

Exercise A. Translate.

1. Discipuli libros multos amant. _____

   _____

2. Christus viros malos judicabit. _____

   _____

3. Lupus pericula non timet. _____

   _____

4. Deus mandata summa dat. _____

   _____

Exercise B. Translate.

1. God loves girls and boys. _____

2. The soldier was carrying a large sword and a shield._____

   _____

3. The angels have harps. _____

4. The Romans were warning the Gauls. _____

Derivatives. Complete these sentences with derivatives from today's lesson.

1. Something that is not optional is _____ .

2. Something that is dangerous is _____ .

3. A man who is very masculine is _____ .

4. An adult who acts childishly is _____ .

5. The head of a school is called a _____ .

6. A rule or basic law is a _____ .

LESSON X

Vocabulary

1.	a, ab	*from, away from,* prep. with abl.
2.	cum	*with,* prep. with abl.
3.	de	*from, down from,* prep. with abl.
4.	in	*in, on,* prep. with abl.
5.	sine	*without,* prep. with abl.
6.	in	*in, into, against,* prep. with acc.
7.	circum	*around, about,* prep. with acc.
8.	ad	*to, near, toward,* prep. with acc.
9.	per	*through,* prep. with acc.
10.	trans	*across,* prep. with acc.

Latin Saying

Hannibal ad portas!

Hannibal at the gates!

Sayings. Translate.

1. Repetitio mater studiorum. _____

2. The master has spoken. _____

3. Nature does not make leaps. _____

4. Per Christum Dominum Nostrum. Amen. _____

   _____

5. ante bellum _____

Grammar

1. Define a *preposition.* _____

2. In Latin the object of a preposition may be in what two cases?

   _____ , _____

3. When the preposition *in* is followed by the accusative case it indicates

   _____ .

4. When *in* is followed by the ablative case it indicates _____ .

Drill A. Translate.

1. cum amicis _____

2. trans agrum _____

3. per januam _____

4. in aqua _____

5. de caelo _____

6. a vicis _____

7. sine scientia _____

8. ad tabernas _____

9. trans culinam _____

Drill B. Translate.

1. through the shield _____

2. without dangers _____

3. in the beginning _____

4. toward the wolf _____

5. into the village _____

6. on the chair _____

7. across the province _____

8. down from the farmhouse _____

9. away from the gate _____

Exercise A. Translate. Prepositional phrases are underlined.

1. Lucia <u>in villa</u> ambulat. _____

_____

2. Marcus <u>in casam</u> ambulabat. _____

_____

3. Agricola <u>sine periculo</u> laborat. _____

_____

4. Pueri et viri <u>circum mundum</u> navigant. _____

_____

Exercise B. Translate. Prepositional phrases are underlined.

1. Farmers and poets live <u>in the village</u>. _____

_____

2. The boys are walking <u>with the girls.</u> _____

_____

3. The sailor sails <u>across the water.</u> _____

_____

4. He is moving the chair <u>toward the table.</u> _____

Vocabulary

First declension nouns

agricola, ae, *m.*	poeta, ae, *m.*
ara, ae	porta, ae
casa, ae	provincia, ae
cithara, ae	scientia, ae
culina, ae	sella, ae
epistula, ae	tabella, ae
fabula, ae	taberna, ae
janua, ae	tuba, ae
Lucia, ae	umbra, ae
natura, ae	villa, ae

Prepositions

ab,a
cum
de
in
sine
in
circum
ad
per
trans

Second declension nouns

	Masculine	*Neuter*
ager, agri	magister, magistri	Evangelium, i
angelus, i	Marcus, i	mandatum, i
apostolus, i	puer, pueri	periculum, i
Christianus, i	Romanus, i	principium, i
Gallus, i	vicus, i	saeculum, i
liber, libri	vir, viri	scutum, i
lupus, i		studium, i

Grammar Forms

Second Declension nouns ending in *er* or *ir*

S.	Pl.	S.	Pl.
ager	agr-i	puer	pueri
agr-i	agr-orum	pueri	puerorum
agr-o	agr-is	puero	pueris
agr-um	agr-os	puerum	pueros
agr-o	agr-is	puero	pueris

Latin Sayings

Retro Satana	Natura non facit saltum	Magister dixit
Repetitio mater studiorum	Hannibal ad portas!	

Drill A. Write each word in the case and number indicated. Translate.

		Case	*Number*		
1.	periculum	dat.	*S.*	_____	_____
2.	janua	gen.	*Pl.*	_____	_____
3.	mandatum	abl.	*Pl.*	_____	_____
4.	vir	dat.	*Pl.*	_____	_____
5.	ager	gen.	*Pl.*	_____	_____
6.	casa	nom.	*Pl.*	_____	_____
7.	saeculum	abl.	*S.*	_____	_____
8.	puer	acc.	*S.*	_____	_____
9.	scutum	acc.	*Pl.*	_____	_____
10.	ara	acc.	*Pl.*	_____	_____

Drill B. Translate.

1. in aquam _____

2. with enthusiasm _____

3. circum terram _____

4. near the Christians _____

5. in casam _____

6. around the chair _____

READING # 2
Roma et Carthago

Roma et Carthago sunt urbes [1]. Roma est in Italia. Carthago est in Africa.
Et Roma et[2] Carthago imperia habent. Carthago in Hispania et Sicilia imperium
habet. Roma in Italia imperium habet. Roma Carthaginem[3] non amat. Carthago
Romam non amat. Carthago multas naves[4] et servos habet. Carthago multam
pecuniam habet. Roma naves non habet. Roma agricolas et milites[5] habet.
Superabitne[6] Carthago Romam?

---

[1] nom. pl of *urbs*
[2] *et....et*, both....and
[3] acc. of *Carthago* (Carthage)
[4] acc. pl. of *navis*
[5] acc. pl of *miles*
[6] *ne* at end of first word in sentence indicates a question

LESSON XI

Grammar Forms

Present tense of sum

	S.		Pl.
sum	*I am*	sumus	*we are*
es	*you are*	estis	*you are*
est	*he, she, it is*	sunt	*they are*

Imperfect tense of sum

	S.		Pl.
eram	*I was*	eramus	*we were*
eras	*you were*	eratis	*you were*
erat	*he, she, it was*	erant	*they were*

Future tense of sum

	S.		Pl.
ero	*I will be*	erimus	*we will be*
eris	*you will be*	eritis	*you will be*
erit	*he, she, it will be*	erunt	*they will be*

Exercise A. Underline the form of the "to be" verb in Latin. Translate sentence into English and underline the "to be" verb in English. Indicate whether it is a linking verb (l.v.) or a helping verb (h.v.). Write the number(s) of these found in each sentence:(1) predicate nominative (2) predicate adjective (3) direct object (4) prepositional phrase.

1. Marcus erat magister. _____

_____

2. Lupi erant soli. _____

_____

3. Galli in agris pugnabant. _____

_____

4. Deus est summus. _____

_____

5. Liber in mensa erat._____

_____

6. Viri erunt legati. _____

_____

7. Marcus cum amicis ambulat._____

_____

8. Epistulae erunt longae. _____

_____

9. Apostoli Christianos in Roma appellabant. _____

_____

10. Christus populum monebat. _____

_____

11. In horto servi erant. _____

_____

12. Christus est Dominus. _____

_____

EXERCISES *for Lesson XI*

Exercise B. Underline the form of the "to be" verb in English.

Indicate whether it is a linking verb (l.v.) or a helping verb (h.v.). Translate sentence into Latin and underline "to be" verb in Latin (if there is one). Write the number(s) of these found in each sentence: (1) predicate nominative (2) predicate adjective (3) direct object (4) prepositional phrase.

1. Mark will be a soldier._____

2. Mary is living in the farmhouse. _____

3. The apostles were holy. _____

4. Caesar was a great general. _____

5. The farmer is in the field. _____

6. The soldier is my brother. _____

7. The farmers are moving the lambs into the field. _____

8. The shops are full. _____

9. The harps are new. _____

10. Lucy was washing the table in the kitchen. _____

11. The battle will be long. _____

12. The battles will be long. _____

Exercise C. For each instruction write two sentences in English and two in Latin.

1. Linking verbs with predicate nouns.

    _____   _____

    _____   _____

2. Linking verbs with predicate adjectives.

    _____   _____

    _____   _____

3. Linking verbs with prepositional phrases.

    _____   _____

    _____   _____

4. Action verbs with helping verbs, *am, is, are, was* or *were.*

    _____   _____

    _____   _____

LESSON XII

Vocabulary

1. voco, vocare, vocavi, vocatus   *call*

2. servo, are, avi, atus   *guard, keep*

3. aro, (1)   *plow*

4. exspecto, (1)   *wait for*

5. tempto, (1)   *tempt*

6. nato, (1)   *swim*

7. erro, (1)   *err*

8. saluto, (1)   *greet*

9. sto, stare, steti, status   *stand*

10. do, dare, dedi, datus   *give*

52

Sayings. Translate.

1. Repetition is the mother of learning. _____

2. Nature does not make leaps. _____

3. Da nobis hodie. _____

4. Magister dixit. _____

5. Pray and work. _____

Grammar

1. The forms from which all other verb forms are derived are called the _____

   _____ .

2. The second principal part in Latin is called the _____ .

3. In English the infinitive is always translated by the verb preceded by the

   preposition _____ .

4. Give the principal parts of

   (a) nato   _____ _____ _____

   (b) porto   _____ _____ _____

   (c) laudo   _____ _____ _____

Drill A. Translate.

1. servabat _____

2. erramus _____

3. eramus _____

4. natabimus _____

5. temptabant _____

6. exspectabunt _____

7. dabant _____

8. arant _____

53

EXERCISES *for Lesson XII*

Drill B. Translate.

1. he will err _____
2. we were swimming_____
3. they guard _____
4. you (s.) are giving_____
5. he will tempt_____
6. you (pl.) will stand _____
   _____

7. he was plowing _____
8. we will greet _____
9. I was guarding _____
10. you (pl.) were waiting for _____
    _____
11. it was tempting _____
12. they will stand_____

Exercise A. Translate.

1. Pueri parvum vicum servabunt. _____
   _____

2. Agricolae proximos agros arant. _____
   _____

3. Viri feminas bonas exspectabant. _____
   _____

4. Pueri et puellae in aqua natabant. _____
   _____

5. Marcus puellam in casa salutat. _____
   _____

Exercise B. Translate. Prepositional phrases are underlined.

1. Angels are guarding the door. _____
2. Mother and Father are standing <u>in the kitchen.</u> _____
   _____
3. My son and my daughter are <u>with friends.</u> _____
   _____
4. Angels do not tempt boys and girls._____
   _____
5. The Romans do not fear danger and war. _____
   _____

LESSON XIII

Vocabulary

1. moneo, monére, monui, monitus   *warn*

2. placeo, ére, ui, itus   *please*

3. valeo, (2)   *am strong, am well*

4. augeo, augére   *increase*

5. caveo, cavére   *guard against, beware of*

6. fleo, flére   *weep*

7. rideo, ridére   *laugh*

8. respondeo, respondére   *answer, reply*

9. maneo, manére   *remain, stay*

10. teneo, tenére   *hold*

Latin Saying

Caveat emptor

Let the buyer beware

Sayings. Translate.

1. To err is human. _____

2. Valete. _____

3. Vale magistra. _____

4. Rident stoldi verba Latina. _____

5. Hannibal at the gates! _____

Grammar

1. Verbs whose infinitive ends in *ére* belong to the _____ conjugation.

2. The endings for the regular principal parts of the second conjugation are

_____

3. Write the principal parts of

(a) valeo _____ _____ _____ _____

(b) habeo _____ _____ _____ _____

(c) debeo _____ _____ _____ _____

Drill A. Translate.

1. cavébit _____

2. tenent _____

3. placébunt _____

4. ridet _____

5. flebant _____

6. placébam _____

7. respondes _____

8. augébis _____

9. valébimus _____

10. manétis _____

EXERCISES *for Lesson XIII*

Drill B. Translate.

1. they will remain _____
2. they were holding _____
3. we will answer _____
4. she weeps _____
5. you (s) are well _____
6. we are laughing _____

7. he was staying _____
8. you (pl) do increase _____
9. I am replying _____
10. I will please _____
11. I was guarding against _____
12. we will hold _____

Exercise A. Translate.

1. Socii Romam cavent. _____
2. Discipulus libros et epistulas tenebat. _____
3. In horto manebit. _____
4. Pueri scientiam in ludo augebant. _____
5. Servi flebant et ridebant. _____

Exercise B. Translate.

1. The farmer guards against the wolf. _____
2. The girls are warning the boys. _____
3. A man will warn a friend. _____
4. The boys and girls in the fields are laughing and crying. _____

_____

Derivatives. Use each derivative in a sentence.

1. tenacious _____
2. ridiculous _____
3. permanent _____
4. respond _____
5. valiant _____

LESSON XIV

Vocabulary

1. ago, agere   *do, drive, act, treat*

2. curro, currere   *run*

3. duco, ducere, duxi, ductus   *lead, guide*

4. bibo, bibere   *drink*

5. rego, regere   *rule*

6. pono, ponere, posui, positus   *put, place, set*

7. trado, tradere   *deliver up, hand over*

8. cado, cadere   *fall*

9. credo, credere   *believe*

10. vivo, vivere   *live*

Grammar Forms

Third conjugation present tense

rego	*I rule*	regimus	*we rule*
regis	*you rule*	regitis	*you rule*
regit	*he, she, it rules*	regunt	*they rule*

Sayings. Translate.

1. Nature does not make leaps. _____

2. Repetition is the mother of learning. _____

3. Gratias tibi ago. _____

4. Miles Christi sum. _____

5. Quo vadis. _____

Grammar

1. Verbs whose infinitive ends in **ere** belong to the _____ conjugation.

2. Give the principal parts of

    (a) **duco** _____ _____ _____ _____

    (b) **pono** _____ _____ _____ _____

3. Conjugate in the present tense:

    (a) **trado** _____ _____   (b) **curro** _____ _____

    _____ _____   _____ _____

    _____ _____   _____ _____

Drill A. Translate.

1. agis _____   7. currunt _____

2. vivunt _____   8. ducis _____

3. cadit _____   9. regitis _____

4. credis _____   10. tradit _____

5. ponitis _____   11. agunt _____

6. bibimus _____   12. credimus _____

EXERCISES *for Lesson XIV*

Drill B. Translate.

1. he drinks _____

2. we lead _____

3. they hand over _____

4. you (s.) live _____

5. you (pl.) act _____

6. I run _____

7. she is falling _____

8. they do place _____

9. we are ruling _____

10. you (s.) are leading _____

11. I am doing _____

12. it puts _____

Exercise A. Translate. Prepositional phrases are underlined.

1. Pueri et puellae <u>in agro</u> currunt. _____

   _____

2. Libri et tabellae <u>de mensa alta</u> cadunt. _____

   _____

3. Imperator provinciam magnam regit. _____

   _____

4. Legatus epistulas multas tradit. _____

Exercise B. Translate. Prepositional phrases are underlined.

1. Christ leads the apostles. _____

2. Mark is running <u>across the field</u>. _____

3. They are placing the table <u>in the cottage</u>. _____

4. Lucy hands over the trumpets and harps. _____

Derivatives. Use each derivative in a sentence.

1. agent _____

2. conduct _____

3. incredible _____

4. cascade _____

5. revive _____

LESSON XV

Vocabulary

1. defendo, defendere — *defend*

2. vinco, vincere, vici, victus — *conquer*

3. edo, edere — *eat*

4. tollo, tollere — *raise (up), take away*

5. cano, canere — *sing*

6. mitto, mittere, misi, missus — *send*

7. scribo, scribere — *write*

8. dico, dicere — *say, tell*

9. claudo, claudere — *shut, close*

10. peto, petere — *seek, beg*

Latin Saying

Arma virumque cano

I sing of arms and a man

—1st line of *Aeneid*

Grammar Forms

Third conjugation imperfect tense

regebam	*I was ruling*	regebamus	*we were ruling*
regebas	*you were ruling*	regebatis	*you were ruling*
regebat	*he, she, it was ruling*	regebant	*they were ruling*

Sayings. Translate.

1. Veni, vidi, vici. _____

2. Agnus Dei, qui tollis peccata mundi. _____

   _____

3. Magister dixit. _____

4. Let the buyer beware. _____

5. I believe in one God. _____

Grammar

1. On blank paper conjugate in the present and imperfect tenses: (a) **vinco** (b) **tollo**

2. Give the principal parts of

   (a) **vinco** _____ _____ _____ _____

   (b) **mitto** _____ _____ _____ _____

Drill A. Translate.

1. petis _____

2. dicit _____

3. edunt _____

4. edebant _____

5. canebatis _____

6. tollebam _____

7. scribunt _____

8. scribebant _____

9. defendebamus _____

10. vincitis _____

11. mittebas _____

12. canit _____

13. scribebat _____

14. tollunt _____

15. petebat _____

Drill B. Translate.

1. I was singing _____

2. you (s.) were conquering _____

3. they are writing _____

4. she does eat _____

5. we were closing _____

6. you (pl.) are sending _____

7. they were begging _____

8. you (s.) take away _____

Exercise A. Translate.

1. Apostoli multas et sanctas epistulas scribebant. _____

   _____

2. Christus peccata tollit. _____

3. Angeli cum citharis et tubis canunt. _____

4. Romani barbaros in Gallia vincebant. _____

Exercise B. Translate.

1. The farmers and poets were eating and drinking in the shop. _____

   _____

2. Mark was closing the door. _____

3. The barbarians are defending Gaul. _____

4. The apostles were writing the Gospels. _____

   _____

Derivatives. Use each derivative in a sentence.

1. dictionary _____

2. edible _____

3. missionary _____

4. petition _____

5. canticle _____

Grammar Forms

First conjugation verbs

aro, (1)
do, dare, dedi, datus
erro, (1)
exspecto, (1)
nato, (1)
saluto, (1)
servo, (1)
sto, stare, steti, status
tempto, (1)
voco, (1)

Second conjugation verbs

augeo, augére
caveo, cavére
fleo, flére
maneo, manére
moneo, monére
placeo, placére
respondeo, respondére
rideo, ridére
teneo, tenére
valeo, valére

Irregular verb *sum*
Present tense

S.	Pl.
sum	sumus
es	estis
est	sunt

Imperfect tense

eram	eramus
eras	eratis
erat	erant

Future tense

ero	erimus
eris	eritis
erit	erunt

Third conjugation verbs

ago, agere	edo, edere
bibo, bibere	mitto, mittere, misi, missus
cado, cadere	peto, petere
cano, canere	pono, ponere, posui, positus
claudo, claudere	rego, regere
credo, credere	scribo, scribere
curro, currere	tollo, tollere
dico, dicere	trado, tradere
defendo, defendere	vinco, vincere, vici, victus
duco, ducere, duxi, ductus	vivo, vivere

Third conjugation

Present tense

rego	regimus
regis	regitis
regit	regunt

Imperfect tense

regebam	regebamus
regebas	rebebatis
regebat	regebant

Latin Sayings

Errare est humanum	caveat emptor
Credo in unum Deum	Arma virumque cano

Drill A. Check the correct tense, number, and person. Translate.

	Tense			Number		Person			Meaning
	Pres.	*Fut.*	*Imp.*	*S.*	*Pl.*	*1*	*2*	*3*	
1. arabimus									
2. stabit									
3. natas									
4. valebunt									
5. ridet									
6. augebam									
7. eritis									
8. currebat									
9. tradebas									
10. cadebant									
11. vivis									
12. vincunt									
13. dicebas									
14. petimus									
15. edebamus									
16. dabo									
17. servabitis									
18. scribebatis									

READING # 3
Lucia et Marcus

Lucia et Marcus in Italia habitabant. Lucia et Marcus in villa in Neapole[1] habitabant. Marcus et Lucia soror et frater erant. Marcus clamabat et pugnabat. Lucia orabat et canebat. Lucia a Marco currebat. Lucia ad villam currebat. Mater et pater in culina cum amicis edebant et bibebant. Lucia per culinam ad agros currebat. Servi in agris arabant. Pastores[2] lupos cavebant. Lucia trans agros ad casam currebat. Magister in casa pueros et puellas docebat. Discipuli in tabellis scribebant. Lucia circum casam currebat ad vicum. Populi in vico ridebant et flebant quod[3] poetae fabulas narrabant. Lucia in sella in taberna sedebat. Lucia erat sola et laeta[4]. Marcus Luciam videt! Marcus eam[5] salutat et sedet. Misera[6] Lucia!

---

[1] Naples
[2] shepherds
[3] because
[4] happy
[5] her
[6] poor (wretched)

LESSON XVI

Vocabulary

1. audio, audire, audivi, auditus — *hear*

2. dormio, ire, ivi, itus — *sleep*

3. munio, (4) — *fortify, construct*

4. impedio, (4) — *hinder, impede*

5. scio, (4) — *know*

6. finio, (4) — *finish, end, limit*

7. punio, (4) — *punish*

8. venio, venire — *come*

9. aperio, aperire — *open*

10. sentio, sentire — *feel, perceive, think*

Latin Saying

Ave Caesar, morituri te salutamus

Hail Caesar, we who are about to die salute you

-- Roman gladiators

Grammar Forms

Fourth conjugation present tense

audio	*I hear*	audimus	*we hear*
audis	*you hear*	auditis	*you hear*
audit	*he, she, it hears*	audiunt	*they hear*

Sayings. Translate.

1. Veni, vidi, vici. _____

2. I sing of arms and a man. _____

3. To err is human._____

4. The mother of Italy - Rome. _____

Grammar

1. Verbs whose infinitives end in **ire** belong to the _____ conjugation.

2. Give the principal parts of

   (a) **munio** _____ _____ _____ _____

   (b) **scio** _____ _____ _____ _____

3. Conjugate in the present tense :

   ____venio____ _____   ____impedio____ _____

   _____ _____   _____ _____

   _____ _____   _____ _____

Drill A. Translate.

1. finis _____

2. venit_____

3. dormiunt _____

4. punitis _____

5. sentimus _____

6. sciunt _____

7. aperit _____

8. punimus _____

9. auditis _____

10. impedis _____

11. munit _____

12. muniunt _____

Drill B. Translate.

1. We are fortifying _____
2. I am coming _____
3. You (s.) do know _____
4. They are finishing _____

5. He does open _____
6. You (pl.) sleep _____
7. He is feeling _____
8. They hinder _____

Exercise A. Translate.

1. Viri ad portam dormiunt. _____

   _____

2. Pueri et viri fabulas audiunt. _____

   _____

3. Puella januam aperit. _____

4. Discipulus tabellam finit. _____

5. Romani in Galliam veniunt. _____

   _____

Exercise B. Translate.

1. The poets know many stories. _____
2. The Romans are punishing the Gauls. _____
3. You are impeding knowledge. _____
4. The farmer is coming around the cottage. _____

Derivatives. Use each derivative in a sentence.

1. impede _____
2. auditorium _____
3. dormitory _____
4. Advent _____
5. punish _____

LESSON XVII

Vocabulary

1.	hodie	*today, this day*
2.	cras	*tomorrow*
3.	heri	*yesterday*
4.	quod	*because*
5.	quis	*who?*
6.	quid	*what?*
7.	ubi	*where?*
8.	cur	*why?*
9.	sed	*but*
10.	nihil	*nothing*

Grammar Forms

Fourth conjugation imperfect tense

audiebam	*I was hearing*	audiebamus	*we were hearing*
audiebas	*you were hearing*	audiebatis	*you were hearing*
audiebat	*he, she, it was hearing*	audiebant	*they were hearing*

Sayings. Translate.

1. Hail Caesar, we who are about to die salute you. _____

   _____

2. The Roman peace. _____

3. The voice of the people is the voice of god. _____

4. Get thee behind me, Satan. _____

5. Repetition is the mother of learning. _____

Grammar

1. Conjugate in the present and imperfect tenses

   dico _____   **dormio** _____

   _____ _____   _____ _____

   _____ _____   _____ _____

   _____ _____   _____ _____

   _____ _____   _____ _____

   _____ _____   _____ _____

Drill A. Translate.

1. Hodie veniunt. _____

2. Heri veniebant. _____

3. Hodie dicis. _____

4. Heri dicebas. _____

5. Hodie dormit. _____

6. Heri dormiebat. _____

7. Hodie finimus. _____

8. Heri finiebamus. _____

EXERCISES *for Lesson XVII*

Drill B. Translate.

1. Tomorrow we will weep. (*fleo*) _____

2. Today we are writing. (*scribo, scribere*) _____

3. Yesterday he was opening. (*aperio*) _____

4. Tomorrow you (s.) will err.(*erro, errare*) _____

5. Today he is plowing. (*aro, arare*) _____

6. Yesterday they were plowing. _____

7. Tomorrow he will guard. (*servo, servare*) _____

8. Today I am laughing. (*rideo*) _____

Exercise A. Translate.

1. Quid agis? _____

2. Poetas amo quod fabulas narrant. _____

   _____

3. Librum amo quod bonus est. _____

4. Cur rides? _____

5. Ubi es? _____

6. Agricola agrum arabat sed poeta canebat. _____

   _____

7. Quid auditis? Nihil audimus. _____

   _____

Exercise B. Translate.

1. Why are you writing on the tablet? _____

2. Who is plowing? _____

3. Who is in the kitchen? _____

4. What is he eating? _____

5. Where is the lamb? _____

LESSON XVIII

Vocabulary

1.	clamor, clamoris	*shouting, shout*
2.	orator, oratoris	*speaker, orator*
3.	senator, senatoris	*senator*
4.	mos, moris, *m.*	*custom*
5.	timor, timoris	*fear*
6.	volúntas, voluntátis	*will, good will*
7.	pastor, pastoris	*shepherd*
8.	virgo, virginis	*virgin*
9.	lectio, lectionis	*lesson*
10.	piscator, piscatoris	*fisherman*

Grammar Forms

Third declension

Masc. and Fem.

S.	Pl.
lex	leg-es
leg-is	leg-um
leg-i	leg-ibus
leg-em	leg-es
leg-e	leg-ibus

Sayings. Translate.

1. The Senate and People of Rome _____

   _____

2. Fiat voluntas tua. _____

3. Hail Caesar, we who are about to die, salute you. _____

   _____

Grammar

1. Nouns whose genitive singular ends in *is* belong to the _____ declension.

2. What is the *natural gender rule*? What declensions does it apply to? _____

   _____

3. Applying the *natural gender rule*, what nouns in today's lesson are masculine? _

   _____ Feminine? _____

4. Applying the *natural gender rule*, what nouns in Lesson IV are masculine? _____

   _____ Feminine? _____

5. Applying the *natural gender rule*, what first declension nouns are masculine?

   _____

6. Applying the *masculine endings rule*, which words in today's lesson are masculine? _____ _____

   In Lesson IV ? _____

7. On blank paper, decline: (a) **mos** (b) **pastor** (c) **miles** (d) **piscator** (e) **clamor**

Drill A. Give the accusative singular and plural in Latin.

1. shepherd _____

2. shout _____

3. lesson _____

4. virgin _____

5. fisherman _____

6. will, good will _____

EXERCISES *for Lesson XVIII*

Drill B. Translate.

1. with the shepherds _____

2. to/for the senator _____

3. without the shepherd _____

4. in the lessons _____

5. of the fears _____

6. to/for the customs _____

7. by/with/from the shouts _____

8. toward the fishermen _____

Exercise A. Translate.

1. Christus piscatores vocabat. _____

_____

2. Pastor agnos ducit. _____

3. Quid senatores in foro dicebant? _____

_____

4. Discipuli lectiones parabunt. _____

_____

5. Romani agricolae erant, non piscatores. _____

_____

Exercise B. Translate.

1. Fears impede the people. (*impedio*) _____

2. Customs guide the people. (*duco*) _____

3. He was walking with the shepherd. _____

4. The Virgin is holy. _____

5. Mark hears the shouts. _____

LESSON XIX

Vocabulary

1.	panis, panis, *m.*	*bread*
2.	custos, custodis	*guard*
3.	tentatio, tentationis	*temptation*
4.	pes, pedis, *m.*	*foot*
5.	dux, ducis	*leader*
6.	libertas, libertatis	*freedom, liberty*
7.	arbor, arboris, *f*	*tree*
8.	sol, solis, *m.*	*sun*
9.	caritas, caritatis	*love, charity*
10.	passio, passionis, *f.*	*suffering*

Latin Saying

Delenda est Carthago

Carthage must be destroyed

—Cato the Elder

Grammar Forms

Third declension Case Endings

Masc. and Fem.

S.	Pl.
--	es
is	um
i	ibus
em	es
e	ibus

Sayings. Translate.

1. Not an orator, not a senator, but a fisherman. _____

2. I sing of arms and a man. _____

3. Nature does not make leaps. _____

4. I believe in one God. _____

Grammar

1. Applying the **natural gender rule**, what words in today's lesson are masculine? _____What wordsare feminine? _____

2. Applying the **masculine endings** rule, what words in today's lesson are masculine? _____What word is an exception? _____

3. Applying the **feminine endings** rule, which words in today's lesson are feminine? _____In Lesson XVIII ? _____

   In lesson IV ? _____

4. On blank paper, decline: **panis, arbor, dux, tentatio, custos**

Drill A. Give case and number, translate.

1. duce _____ ____ _____

2. custodi _____ ____ _____

3. panem _____ ____ _____

4. solum _____ ____ _____

5. cum caritate _____ ____ _____

6. tentationibus _____ ____ _____

7. pedum _____ ____ _____

8. arborum _____ ____ _____

EXERCISES *for Lesson XIX*

Drill B. Translate.

1. without suffering _____

2. in the trees _____

3. to/for bread _____

4. of leaders _____

5. temptations _____

6. toward liberty _____

7. across the sun _____

8. around the feet _____

Exercise A. Translate.

1. Lucia panem in mensa ponit. _____

   _____

2. Christus libertatem dat. _____

   _____

3. Luna circum terram movet. _____

   _____

4. Terra circum solem movet. _____

   _____

5. Custodes januas claudebant. _____

   _____

Exercise B. Translate.

1. The trees move in the wind. _____

2. The apostles were having temptations and sufferings. _____

   _____

3. The leaders and senators praise liberty. _____

   _____

4. The sun was moving across the sky. _____

Derivatives. Use each derivative in a sentence.

1. solar _____

2. companion _____

3. pedal _____

4. custodian _____

LESSON XX

Vocabulary

1.	avis, avis, *f.*	*bird, sign, omen*
2.	ovis, ovis, *f.*	*sheep*
3.	orbis, orbis, *m.*	*world, orbit, circle*
4.	mens, mentis, *f.*	*mind, understanding*
5.	ars, artis, *f.*	*art, skill*
6.	nix, nivis, *f.*	*snow*
7.	finis, finis, *m.*	*end, boundary*
8.	dens, dentis, *m.*	*tooth*
9.	sedes, sedis, *f.*	*seat, abode*
10.	civis, civis, *m. or f.*	*citizen*

Latin Saying

Romanus civis sum

I am a citizen of Rome

Grammar Forms

Third declension *i-stem* nouns

S.	*Pl.*
pars	part-es
part-is	part-<u>ium</u>
part-i	part-ibus
part-em	part-es
part-e	part-ibus

Sayings. Translate.

1. Today Christ is born. _____

2. Carthage must be destroyed. _____

3. Let the buyer beware. _____

4. In the year of Our Lord. _____

Grammar

1. Third declension nouns that have an **i** in the genitive plural are called

_____ .

2. On blank paper, decline: **dens, sedes, ovis**

3. On blank paper, decline (a) **bad leader** (b) **good law**

Drill A. Translate.

1. cum civibus _____

2. in nive _____

3. circum orbem _____

4. sine arte _____

5. dentes _____

6. sedes _____

7. avium _____

8. ovi _____

9. mente _____

10. finem _____

11. civium _____

12. avi _____

Drill B. Translate.

1. many birds _____
2. small sheep _____
3. of the arts _____
4. of the birds _____

5. with the sheep _____
6. by/with/from the seat _____
7. toward the end _____
8. the great minds _____

Exercise A. Translate.

1. Cives in nive cadunt. _____
2. Aves dentes non habent. _____
3. Pastores oves ducebant. _____
4. Quid oratores dicunt? _____
5. Poetae cum arte canunt. _____

Exercise B. Translate.

1. The shepherds were defending the sheep. _____

   _____

2. The citizens were always looking at birds. _____

   _____

3. Snow is falling down from the sky. _____
4. The boy has a bad tooth. _____

Derivatives. Use each derivative in a sentence.

1. aviation _____
2. artistic _____
3. dental _____
4. civil _____
5. mental _____

Fourth conjugation verbs

aperio, aperire
audio, (4)
dormio, (4)
finio (4)
impedio, (4)
munio, (4)
punio, (4)
scio, (4)
sentio, sentire
venio, venire

Other words

cras
cur
heri
hodie
nihil
quid
quis
quod
sed
ubi

Fourth conjugation present tense

audio	audimus
audis	auditis
audit	audiunt

imperfect tense

audiebam	audiebamus
audiebas	audiebatis
audiebat	audiebant

Third declension nouns
Masculine and feminine

"ium" nouns

arbor, arboris, *f.*
caritas, caritatis
clamor, clamoris
custos, custodis
dux, ducis
lectio, lectionis
libertas, libertatis
mos, moris *m.*
orator, oratoris
panis, panis, *m.*

passio, passionis, *f.*
pastor, pastoris
pes, pedis, *m.*
piscator, piscatoris
senator, senatoris
sol, solis, *m.*
tentatio, tentationis
timor, timoris
virgo, virginis
voluntas, voluntatis

ars, artis, *f.*
avis, avis, *f.*
civis, civis, *c.*
dens, dentis, *m.*
finis, finis, *m.*
mens, mentis, *f.*
nix, nivis, *f.*
orbis, orbis, *m.*
ovis, ovis, *f.*
sedes, sedis, *f.*

Third declension noun forms
Case endings
Masculine and feminine

S.	Pl.	S.	Pl.	S.	Pl.
lex	leges	-	es	pars	partes
legis	legum	is	**(i)um**	partis	part**ium**
legi	legibus	i	ibus	parti	partibus
legem	leges	em	es	partem	partes
lege	legibus	e	ibus	parte	partibus

Latin Sayings

Ave Caesar, morituri te salutamus
Romanus civis sum
Non oratorem, non senatorem, sed piscatorem

Hodie Christus natus est
Delenda est Carthago

Drill A. Give the correct form of the verb. Translate.

		Tense	*Person*	*Number*	
1.	venio	pres.	3	S.	_____
2.	finio	imp.	2	Pl.	_____
3.	munio	pres.	1	Pl.	_____
4.	punio	imp.	3	Pl.	_____
5.	scio	pres.	2	S.	_____

Drill B. Give the nominative and genitive singular and gender.

1. tooth _____ _____ _____
2. fear _____ _____ _____
3. lesson _____ _____ _____
4. freedom _____ _____ _____
5. suffering _____ _____ _____
6. bread _____ _____ _____
7. seat _____ _____ _____
8. mind _____ _____ _____
9. guard _____ _____ _____
10. sun _____ _____ _____

READING # 4
Caesar

Galli et Romani semper pugnabant. Galli erant barbari. Romani erant cives. Senatus Populusque Romanus Caesarem in Galliam mittebant. Caesar Gallos puniebat quod trans finem provinciae[1] veniebant. Caesar et milites in Galliam veniebant. Caesar Romam et imperium Romanum defendebat. Galli fortes[2] erant sed Caesar eos[3] vincebat. Galli magnum ducem habebant sed Caesar eum[4] vincebat. Caesar ad Britianniam[5] navigabat sed Britianniam non vincebat. Caesar autem[6] imperator summus erat. Caesar orator et imperator et scriptor[7] magnus erat. Laudasne[8] Caesarem?

---

[1] boundary of the province
[2] brave
[3] them
[4] him
[5] Britain
[6] however
[7] writer
[8] *ne* at end of first word of sentence indicates a question

LESSON XXI

Vocabulary

1. iter, itineris, *n.*   *journey, march, route*

2. vulnus, vulneris   *wound*

3. sal, salis   *salt, sea water*

4. mare, maris   *sea*

5. carmen, carminis, *n.*   *song*

6. cor, cordis, *n.*   *heart*

7. rus, ruris   *countryside*

8. ver, veris, *n.*   *spring (season)*

9. opus, óperis   *work, deed*

10. flumen, fluminis, *n.*   *river*

Grammar Forms

Third declension neuter

S.	Pl.
flumen	flumin-a
flumin-is	flumin-um
flumin-i	flumin-ibus
flumen	flumin-a
flumin-e	flumin-ibus

Sayings. Translate.

1. I am a citizen of Rome. _____

2. Hannibal at the gates! _____

3. Not an orator, not a senator, but a fisherman. _____

_____

4. Work conquers all. _____

Grammar

1. Applying the **neuter endings** rule, which words in today's lesson are neuter ?

_____   _____   In Lesson IV? _____

_____

2. On blank paper, decline: **carmen**, **vulnus**, **opus**, **cor**, **miles** (masc.)

3. On blank paper, decline (a) **deep river**(b) **long journey**

Drill A. Give the accusative singular and plural.

1. flumen _____   3. opus _____

2. cor _____   4. vulnus _____

Drill B. Translate.

1. magnum opus _____

2. plenum cor _____

3. multa carmina _____

4. trans rus _____

5. per flumina _____

6. vulnere _____

7. sine multis vulneribus _____

8. in sale _____

Drill C. Translate.

1. to/for the hearts _____

2. journeys _____

3. in the deep river _____

4. through the deep river _____

5. in the deep sea _____

6. of the good songs _____

7. of the good song _____

8. to/for the new works _____

_____

Exercise A. Translate.

1. Iter est longum. _____

2. Vulnera erant mala. _____

3. Milites trans multa flumina veniebant. _____

_____

4. Milites multa vulnera habent sed pugnant. _____

_____

5. Multi milites sunt in itinere. _____

_____

Exercise B. Translate.

1. The poet sings without heart. _____

2. The poets sing many songs. _____

3. The soldiers are fighting in the river. _____

_____

4. The boys and girls are waiting for spring. _____

_____

Derivatives. Use each derivative in a sentence.

1. rural _____

2. invulnerable _____

3. itinerary _____

4. cordial _____

Vocabulary

1.	undique	*on (from) all sides*
2.	statim	*at once, immediately*
3.	os, oris, *n.*	*mouth*
4.	itaque	*therefore*
5.	autem	*however*
6.	etiam	*also, even*
7.	tum	*then, at that time*
8.	jus, juris, *n.*	*right*
9.	diu	*for a long time*
10.	fons, fontis, *m.* (i-stem)	*fountain, spring, source*

Latin Saying

Etiam capillus unus habet umbram

Even one hair has a shadow

—Publius Syrus

Grammar Forms

CASE ENDINGS
Third declension neuter

	S.	*Pl.*
	--	a
	is	um
	i	ibus
	--	a
	e	ibus

Sayings. Translate.

1. O the times, O the customs _____

2. my fault _____

3. I am a citizen of Rome _____

4. wonder of the world _____

Grammar

1. In Latin, neuter nouns of any declension, singular and plural, always have the same endings for what two cases? _____, _____

2. On blank paper, decline: **fons**, **jus**, **os**

Drill A. Translate.

1. jura _____

2. fontium _____

3. oribus _____

4. diu _____

5. undique _____

6. etiam _____

7. juribus _____

8. fonti _____

Drill B. Give the following forms.

1. *dative singular*: amicus _____, os _____,
   panis _____, stella _____,
   gaudium _____

2. *genitive singular*: ventus _____, puella _____,
   jus _____, lex _____, studium _____

3. *ablative plural*: puer _____, casa _____,
   mandatum _____, fons _____, timor _____

Exercise A. Translate.

1. Tum milites undique veniebant. _____

   _____

2. Senatores timores multos habent, manent autem. _____

   _____

3. Etiam fons aquam non habet. _____

   _____

4. Magister docebat, discipulus autem os aperiebat. _____

   _____

Exercise B. Translate.

1. Immediately the general seeks peace. _____

   _____

2. The citizens seek peace, however the generals prepare war. _____

   _____

3. The fountains will have much water. _____

   _____

4. The guards were standing at the gates for a long time. _____

   _____

Derivatives. Use each derivative in a sentence.

1. oral _____

2. jury _____

3. juror _____

4. fountain _____

Vocabulary

1.	adventus, us	*coming, arrival*
2.	equitatus, us	*cavalry*
3.	exercitus, us	*army*
4.	portus, us	*harbor*
5.	senatus, us	*senate*
6.	spiritus, us	*spirit*
7.	fructus, us	*fruit, profit, enjoyment*
8.	usus, us	*use, experience*
9.	lacus, us	*lake, pit*
10.	impetus, us	*attack*

Latin Saying

O praeclarum custodem ovium lupum.

O, excellent protector of sheep, the wolf.

—Cicero

Grammar

Fourth Declension

Noun Forms				Case Endings	
S.	*Pl.*			*S.*	*Pl.*
port-us	port-us			us	us
port-us	port-uum			us	uum
port-ui	port-ibus			ui	ibus
port-um	port-us			um	us
port-u	port-ibus			u	ibus

Sayings. Translate.

1. Even one hair has a shadow. _____

2. Gloria Patri et Filio et Spiritui Sancto_____

   _____

3. always faithful_____

4. I sing of arms and a man. _____

Grammar

1. Nouns whose genitive singular ending is *us* belong to the declension._____

2. Most fourth declension nouns are _____ in gender.

3. On a separate piece of paper, decline: (a) **equitatus** (b) **usus** (c) **deep lake**

Drill A. Give the accusative singular and plural of these fourth declension nouns.

1. fructus   _____   _____

2. equitatus   _____   _____

3. usus   _____   _____

4. impetus   _____   _____

Drill B. Translate.

1. fructuum _____

2. adventum _____

3. portibus _____

4. sine equitatu _____

5. a lacu _____

6. de portu _____

7. ad exercitum _____

8. impetum _____

9. in spiritu _____

10. cum senatu _____

11. lacibus _____

12. usibus _____

C. Translate.

1. around the lake _____

2. through the harbors _____

3. into the cavalry _____

4. with the army _____

5. of the harbors _____

6. to/for the arrival _____

7. by/with/from experience _____

8. across the lake _____

Exercise A. Translate.

1. Imperator exercitum circum lacum ducebat. _____

2. Senatus adventum expectabit. _____

3. Agricolae fructus ad portum portabunt. _____

4. Imperator impetum prohibebat. _____

Exercise B. Translate.

1. The army is coming near Carthage. _____

2. The cavalry is coming from all sides. _____

3. Christ sends the Holy Spirit. _____

4. The general leads the large army. _____

Derivatives. Use each derivative in a sentence.

1. impetuous _____

2. advent _____

3. adventure _____

4. equestrian _____

LESSON XXIV

Vocabulary

1. dies, diei, *m.*   *day*

2. acies, ei   *battle line*

3. fides, ei   *faith, loyalty*

4. res, ei   *thing*

5. spes, ei   *hope*

6. meridies, ei, *m.*   *midday, noon*

7. facies, ei   *face*

Latin Saying

> **Dies Irae**
>
> *Day of Wrath*

Grammar

Fifth Declension

Noun Forms		Case Endings	
S.	*Pl.*	*S.*	*Pl.*
r-es	r-es	es	es
r-ei	r-erum	ei	erum
r-ei	r-ebus	ei	ebus
r-em	r-es	em	es
r-e	r-ebus	e	ebus

Sayings. Translate.

1. Sign of the cross _____

2. Even one hair has a shadow. _____

3. O excellent protector of sheep, the wolf! _____

   _____

4. Tibi gratias ago. _____

Grammar

1. Nouns whose genitive singular ends in **ei** belong to the _____ declension.

2. Most nouns of the fifth declension are _____ in gender.

   Two exceptions are _____ and _____ .

3. On blank paper, decline: (a) **spes**   (b) **dies bonus**   (c) **facies nova**

Drill A. Give the accusative singular and plural.

1. dies _____   _____

2. spes _____   _____

3. res _____   _____

4. facie _____   _____

Drill B. Translate.

1. in longam aciem _____

2. sancta fides _____

3. per spem _____

4. sine multis rebus _____

5. ab acie _____

6. post meridiem (P.M.) _____

7. bonarum rerum _____

8. multis bonis diebus _____

EXERCISES *for Lesson XX IV*

Drill C. Translate.

1. to/for many good things _____

5. without days _____

_____

_____

2. (by) faith alone _____

6. without faith _____

3. of faces _____

7. your face _____

4. without hope _____

8. of new things _____

Exercises A. Translate.

1. Deus bonas et multas res parat. _____

_____

2. Christiani fidem et spem habent. _____

_____

3. Miles in acie longa pugnabat. _____

_____

4. Puella faciem novam habet. _____

_____

Exercise B. Translate.

1. My face warns the student. _____

2. The cavalry is coming into the battle line. _____

_____

3. God gives hope. _____

4. The days are long. _____

Derivatives. Use each derivative in a sentence.

1. fidelity _____

2. facial _____

3. despair _____

4. meridian _____

LESSON XXV

Vocabulary

1. clarus, a, um   *clear, bright, famous*

2. cupidus, a, um   *eager, desirous*

3. laetus, a, um   *glad, joyful, happy*

4. Christianus, a, um   *Christian*

5. Romanus, a, um   *Roman*

6. albus, a, um   *white*

7. alienus, a, um   *unfavorable, foreign*

8. almus, a , um   *nurturing, kindly*

9. verus, a, um   *true*

10. beatus, a, um   *blessed*

Latin Saying

Deo gratias

Thanks be to God

Sayings. Translate.

1. Day of wrath _____

2. O excellent protector of sheep, the wolf! _____

   _____

3. O the times, O the customs _____

4. nurturing mother _____

Drill A. Translate.

1. clarus vir _____

2. clara femina _____

3. laeti viri _____

4. laetae feminae _____

5. agnus albus _____

6. alienus hostis _____

7. almi amici _____

8. vera fides _____

9. Beata Virgo Maria _____

10. vicus Romanus _____

11. laetus poeta _____

12. Christianae virtutes _____

Drill B. Translate.

1. foreign tribe _____

2. kindly heart _____

3. Christian faith _____

4. Roman gods _____

5. blessed year _____

6. true hope _____

7. true heart _____

8. nurturing faith _____

9. white snow _____

10. white sheep (pl.) _____

11. foreign guard _____

12. eager boy _____

Exercise A. Translate.

1. Christiani Veram Fidem habent. _____

2. Quid Christianae virtutes sunt? Christianae virtutes sunt Fides, Spes, et Caritas.

   _____

   _____

3. Miles cor cupidum habet. _____

4. Poetae carmen laetum amant. _____

Exercise B. Translate.

1. Christians will be blessed and happy with Jesus in heaven. _____

   _____

2. The journey was long, but happy. _____

   _____

3. Roman wars are famous. _____

4. The Romans were staying with foreign tribes. _____

   _____

Derivatives. Use each derivative in a sentence.

1. Cupid _____

2. albino _____

3. verify _____

4. alien _____

5. clarify _____

Grammar Forms

Third declension
neuter

carmen, carminis
cor, cordis,
flumen, fluminis
iter, itineris
jus, juris
mare, maris
opus, operis
os, oris
rus, ruris
ver, veris
vulnus, vulneris

masculine
fons, fontis
sal, salis

Sayings

O Tempora, O mores
Dies Irae
Deo gratias
Etiam capillus unus habet umbram
O praeclarum custodem ovium lupum

Fourth declension

adventus, us
equitatus, us
exercitus, us
fructus, us
impetus, us
lacus, us
portus, us
senatus, us
spiritus, us
usus, us

Other words

autem
diu
etiam
itaque
tatim
tum
undique

Fifth declension

acies, aciei
dies, diei, *m.*
facies, faciei
fides, fidei
meridies, ei, *m.*
res, rei
spes, spei

Adjectives

albus, a, um
alienus, a, um
almus, a, um
beatus, a, um
Christianus, a, um
clarus, a, um
cupidus, a, um
laetus, a, um
Romanus, a, um
verus, a, um

Third Declension
neuter forms

S.	Pl.
flumen	flumina
fluminis	fluminum
flumini	fluminibus
flumen	flumina
flumine	fluminibus

Third Declension
neuter case endings

S.	Pl.
—	a
is	um
i	ibus
—	a
e	ibus

Fourth Declension
forms and case endings

S.	Pl.
port-us	port-us
port-us	port-uum
port-ui	port-ibus
port-um	port-us
port-u	port-ibus

Fifth Declension
forms and case endings

S.	Pl.
r-es	r-es
r-ei	r-erum
r-ei	r-ebus
r-em	r-es
r-e	r-ebus

Drill A. Give the correct form for each noun and translate.

		case/number	form	translation
1.	flumen	dat. Pl.		
2.	fides	abl. S.		
3.	spiritus	gen. Pl.		
4.	jus	acc. Pl.		
5.	ver	nom. Pl.		
6.	lacus	abl. Pl.		
7.	usus	gen. S.		
8.	acies	dat. S.		
9.	os	acc. S.		
10.	sal	dat. S.		

READING # 5
Christiani et Romani

Romani Christianos diu non amabant. Christiani Christum et Deum et Spiritum Sanctum adorabant. Christiani carmina in ecclesia canebant. Christiani in ecclesia panem edebant et vinum bibebant. Christiani veritatem credebant et docebant. Christiani fidem in Christo non in Caesare ponebant. Christiani Caesarem non adorabant.

Romani Christianos puniebant. Erat magna ignis in Roma. Nero, imperator Romanus, Christianos appellabat. "Habetis culpam," inquit[1]. Christiani autem Neronem[2] non timebant quod in Christo fidem ponebant. Nero in Colliseum Christianos jubebat. Leones[3] in Colliseum veniebant. Christiani autem leones non timebant. Christiani orabant et in carminibus Christum laudabant. Christiani pro[4] Christo vitas dabant. Christiani erant laeti et beati. Christiani nunc in Caelo sunt. Laudasne[5] Christianos aut[6] Romanos?

---

[1] he said
[2] acc. of Nero
[3] nom. pl. of leo
[4] for
[5] ne at end of first word indicates a question
[6] or

Appendices

Selections for Memorization

Selections for memorization give students exposure to real Latin and also provide future texts for translation and illustration of syntax. In addition, these selections expose students to their religious, cultural, and musical heritage. The *Gloria, Sanctus, Gloria Patri*, and *Ave Maria* may be more readily learned by singing in Gregorian chant or listening to music recordings if so desired.

The first two selections are from the Ordinary of the Mass. The Ordinary of the Mass is the part with unchanging text and consists of five parts:

> Kyrie (Lord have mercy)
> Gloria (Glory to God in the highest)
> Credo (The Nicene Creed, beginning, *I believe in one God*)
> Sanctus and Benedictus (Holy, Holy, Holy)
> Agnus Dei ((Lamb of God)

The techniques of harmony and counterpoint, the basis of all European music, came directly from improvising on the singing of the Mass in plainchant. As composers continued to develop musical technique, their primary text was the Ordinary of the Mass in Latin, which became the inspiration for more musical masterpieces than any other source. The great Viennese masters Haydn, Mozart and Schubert wrote some of their most glorious music in their masses. Some of the most famous Masses are Bach's *B-minor Mass*, Beethoven's *Missa Solemnis* and Mozart's *Requiem Mass*.   Since the Catholic Church has discarded much of its traditional music, the world has picked it up and now many Protestant and secular music groups perform Gregorian chant, Masses, and other Latin music as part of their cultural and religious heritage.

*The **Gloria** is the Church's great hymn of praise.*

Gloria

Gloria in excelsis Deo	*Glory to God in the highest*
Et in terra pax hominibus bonae voluntatis	*And on earth peace to men of good will.*
Laudamus te, Benedicimus te	*We praise you, we bless you*
Adoramus te, Glorificamus te	*We worship you, we glorify you*
Gratias agimus tibi	*We give you thanks*
Propter magnam gloriam tuam	*because of your great glory*
Domine Deus, Rex caelestis	*Lord God, Heavenly King*
Deus Pater omnipotens.	*Almighty God and Father.*
Domine Fili unigenite Jesu Christe	*Lord Jesus Christ, Only Begotten Son*
Domine Deus, Agnus Dei, Filius Patris	*Lord God, Lamb of God, Son of the Father*
Qui tollis peccata mundi, miserere nobis	*You take away the sins of the world, have mercy on us.*
Qui tollis peccata mundi,	*You take away the sins of the world,*
Suscipe deprecationem nostram.	*Receive our prayer.*
Qui sedes ad dexteram Patris,	*You are seated at the right hand of the Father*
miserere nobis. Quoniam tu solus sanctus.	*Have mercy on us. For you alone are holy*
Tu solus Dominus. Tu solus Altissimus,	*You alone are Lord. You alone are the most high*
Jesu Christe, cum Sancto Spiritu,	*Jesus Christ,with the Holy Spirit*
in gloria Dei Patris. Amen	*in the glory of God the Father. Amen*

Sanctus

Sanctus, Sanctus, Sanctus,	*Holy, holy, holy,*
Dominus Deus Sabaoth	*Lord God of Hosts*
Pleni sunt Caeli et Terra, gloria tua	*Heaven and earth are full of Your glory*
Hosanna in excelsis	*Hosanna in the highest*
Benedictus qui venit in nomine Domini	*Blessed is he who comes in the name of the Lord*
Hosanna in excelsis	*Hosanna in the highest*

*A doxology is a hymn of praise to the Trinity. This doxology is also called the **Glory be** or **Gloria Patri**, according to the custom of naming a prayer after its first two words.*

Doxology
(Glory be)

Gloria Patri, et Filio, et Spiritui Sancto	*Glory be to the Father, Son, and Holy Spirit*
Sicut erat in principio et nunc,	*As it was in the beginning, is now*
Et semper et in saecula saeculorum. Amen.	*And ever shall be, world without end. Amen.*

*There are many beautiful versions of the Ave Maria. The most famous, by Franz Schubert, scandalized many listeners the first time it was sung in church because of its theatrical style. Schubert's **Ave Maria** is often called the world's most beautiful song, a fitting tribute to the most honored and revered woman in history, whom William Wordsworth called "our tainted nature's solitary boast."*

Ave Maria

Ave Maria, gratia plena	*Hail Mary, full of grace*
Dominus tecum,	*The Lord is with thee*
Benedicta tu in mulieribus	*Blessed art thou among women*
Et benedictus fructus ventris tui, Jesus	*And blessed is the fruit of thy womb, Jesus*
Sancta Maria, Mater Dei	*Holy Mary, Mother of God*
Ora pro nobis peccatoribus	*Pray for us sinners*
Nunc et in hora mortis nostrae. Amen.	*Now and at the hour of our death. Amen.*

Scripture Passage Translation

How many of these words do you know or can you figure out? Words learned in this course are underlined.

Genesis 1:1-5

<u>In principio</u> creavit <u>Deus caelum et terram</u>. <u>Terra autem erat</u> inanis et vacua et

tenebrae <u>super faciem</u> abyssi <u>et spiritus Dei</u> ferebatur <u>super aquas</u>. Dixitque [1]

<u>Deus:</u> "Fiat <u>lux</u>." Et facta est <u>lux</u>. <u>Et vidit Deus lucem quod</u> esset <u>bona et</u> divisit

<u>lucem</u> ac tenebras. <u>Appellavitque</u> <u>lucem diem</u> et tenebras <u>noctem</u>. Factumque est

vespere et mane <u>dies unus.</u>

John 1:1-5

<u>In principio erat Verbum et Verbum erat</u> apud <u>Deum et Deus erat Verbum</u>.

Hoc <u>erat in principio</u> apud <u>Deum</u>. Omnia <u>per</u> ipsum facta <u>sunt et sine</u> ipso

factum est <u>nihil.</u> Quod factum est in ipso <u>vita erat et vita erat lux hominum et</u>

<u>lux in</u> tenebris lucet et tenebrae eam non compehenderunt.

[1] **que** added to the end of a word means *and* , also notice **appelavitque** and **factumque** in line 4

Optime!	*Excellent*
Pessime!	*Very bad!*
I (ite, pl.) ad januam	*Go to the door*
fenestram	*window*
tabulam nigram	*blackboard*
Aperi	*Open*
Claude	*Close*
januam	*door*
fenestram	*window*
librum	*book*
Aperite libros	*Open (your) books*
Me paenitet	*I'm sorry*
Fiat	*All right (let it be done)*
De hoc satis	*Enough of this!*
Collige folia	*Collect the papers*
Ego amo te	*I love you*
Quid dixit	*What did he say?*

Veni Veni Emmanuel

This hymn actually traces its origins to the church liturgy prior to the ninth century. The text is derived from the seven great O antiphons which were said at vespers from Dec 17 to Dec 23. The first English translation appeared in 1851 and it is now a popular Christmas carol, sung in both English and Latin.

Plainsong, 12th Century

Veni Creator Spiritus

This is a vesper hymn for Whitsunday (Pentecost) by Rabanus Maurus, Archbishop of Mainz (d. 856). It is sung at other solemn occasions such as ordinations and dedications of Churches. It is also a traditional hymn for the opening of the school year at academic institutions.

Ve - ni, Cre - a - tor Spi - ri - tus,
Qui di - ce - - - ris Pa - - ra - cli - tus,

Men - tes tu - o - rum vi - si - ta: Im - ple su - per - na gra - ti - a
Al - tis - si - mi do - num de - i, Fons vi - vus, ig - nis, ca - ri - tas

Quae tu cre - a - sti pec - to - ra. A - - - men.
Et spi - ri - ta - lis unc - ti - o.

Gaudeamus Igitur

Music was an important part of life in medieval Europe, not only in churches, but also in taverns, villages, schools, castles and roadsides. This is the greatest of the medieval student songs, and a jollier, more rousing song would be hard to find. Brahms used its melody in the glorious climax to his "Academic Festival Overture."

GAUDEAMUS IGITUR
Let us rejoice therefore,
while we are young
After delightful youth
After a hard old age
The earth will have us
The earth will have us

Long live the university
Long live the professors
Long live all the graduates
Long live all the undergraduates
May they ever flourish
May they ever flourish

Long live the republic
And those who rule it
Long live our state
Long live this association
Which gathers us to this place
Which gathers us to this place

VENI CREATOR SPIRITUS[1]
Come Creator Spirit
visit the souls of thy people,
fill with grace from on high
the hearts which thou hast created

Thou who art called the Comforter,
gift of the most high God,
living fount, fire, love
and unction of souls.

VENI VENI EMMANUEL
O Come, O come, Emmanuel,
And ransom captive Israel,
That mourns in lonely exile here
Until the son of God appear.
Rejoice, rejoice, Emmanuel
Shall come to thee, O Israel.

O come, thou Rod of Jesse, free
Thine own from Satan's tyranny,
From depths of hell thy people save
And give them victory o're the grave.
Rejoice, rejoice, Emmanuel
Shall come to thee, O Israel.

[1] translation by Adrian Fortescue

History Questions

Questions with an asterisk are not completely answered in *Famous Men of Rome*.

CHAPTER 14

1. What were the three wars with Carthage called?
2. What does the word *Punic* mean?
*3. How long did it take Rome to conquer and unify most of Italy?
4. What military advantage did Carthage have over Rome?
*5. Contrast the economies of Rome and Carthage.
*6. Contrast the religions of Rome and Carthage.
7. What piece of land was the First Punic War fought over?
8. How did Regulus become a prisoner of Carthage?
9. What two things did Regulus value over his own life?

CHAPTER 15

1. Where did the Second Punic War begin?
2. How did Scipio make the Spaniards allies of Rome?
3. What great obstacle did Hannibal cross to reach Italy?
*4. Why did Hannibal always defeat the Roman generals in battles? What special weapon did he have?
5. What is a Fabian policy and how did it get its name?
6. Where was Hannibal's greatest victory?
7. Why did Hannibal go back to Carthage?
8. What offer did Hannibal make to Scipio before the battle of Zama?
9. Who did Hannibal think were the three greatest generals that had ever lived?
*10. Carthage was led by one of the greatest generals in history who invaded Italy and came near to the gates of Rome. Why didn't Hannibal take the city of Rome and why did Carthage ultimately lose the Second Punic War?

CHAPTER 16

1. Why is Cato called Cato the Censor? Describe his personality?
2. How did Cato end every speech in the Senate?
3. What unreasonable demand did Rome make of Carthage that caused the Third Punic War?
4. Rome's struggle with Carthage covered what time period?

CHAPTER 17

1. Who was the mother of the Gracchi and what did she call her sons?
2. How had the patricians been unjust to the plebeians?
3. What law did Tiberius Gracchus get passed that caused the nobles to hate him?
*4. Who was elected tribune after Tiberius was killed?
5. What falsehood did the nobles spread about both of the Gracchi?
6. Why did Caius Gracchus ask his slave to kill him?

CHAPTER 18

1. After the Gracchi were both killed, what great man came forward as champion of the plebeians?
2. Why were the nobles unable to get rid of Marius?
3. What three barbarian tribes threatened Rome and where were they from?
*4. Contrast the fighting style of the barbarians and the Romans.
5. What did the Cimbri ask of Marius and what was his reply?
6. What was the Social War and what general gained fame from it?
7. In what war did the Senate appoint Sulla commander, and the tribunes appoint Marius commander?
8. What did Marius tell a solider to tell to the Roman governor of Africa?
9. How did Marius regain control of Rome and what did he do?

CHAPTER 19

1. Who was aiding the Greeks in their rebellion against Rome?
2. Why was Athens so difficult to conquer?
3. What weapon did Sulla use to break down the walls of Athens?
4. Who was in control of Rome when Sulla returned from his war against the Greeks?
5. Describe Sulla's "Reign of Terror" and his Triumph?
6. What did Sulla do when he tired of being dictator?

CHAPTER 20

1. What did the "sea rovers" or pirates do and where were they from?
2. How did Pompey defeat them?
3. Why was Pompey so popular with the people, even though he was a dictator?
4. Was Pompey a friend of the Marians or Sulla?

CHAPTER 21

1. Why was Julius Caesar the greatest Roman of all?
2. Who was Caesar's aunt?
3. What did Sulla say about Caesar?
4. Was Caesar a friend of the nobles or the plebeians?
5. What was Caesar's first important political appointment?
6. How many men were in a legion?
7. What bird was on the military standard of the legions?
*8. What large area of Europe did Caesar conquer and bring into the Roman Empire? How long did it take him? What is the name of his military journal of this war?
9. Who was the ruler of Rome when Caesar was ready to return after his conquest of Gaul?
10. What did Pompey do when Caesar refused to disband his armies, as Pompey had ordered?

11. What river on the southern boundary of Gaul did Caesar cross to enter into Italy?

12. Where did the armies of Pompey and Caesar meet?

13. Where was Pompey killed and by whom?

14. Some of the nobles and senators formed an army which was defeated by Caesar in Asia Minor. What famous dispatch did Caesar send to the Senate after this victory?

15. After Caesar defeated all of his enemies and was made dictator for life, what title showed that he was in command of all of the armies of the Empire?

16. How was the Julian calendar an improvement over the one it replaced?

17. What warning was given to Caesar by an augur who stopped him on the way to the Forum?

18. The most highly respected of the conspirators was also a personal friend of Caesar. Who was he?

19. How did the assassins of Caesar defend their actions to the people?

20. What famous Roman made an eloquent speech at Caesar's funeral?

*A. How did Caesar increase his popularity with the people?
   Is vote buying a problem in all democracies and republics?

*B. What does the expression "he has crossed the Rubicon" mean?

*C. Why did the death of Caesar fail to "save the Republic"?

*D. Is it possible for a nation to be a Republic and have an Empire at the same time? Why?
   Which is better?

*E. Is the conflict between republican government and empire building applicable to America? Explain.

CHAPTER 22

1. Who was one of the greatest orators in the history of Rome?

2. What mysterious conspiracy to overthrow Rome was defeated by Cicero's eloquent and powerful speeches in the Senate?

*3. These speeches are considered to be the greatest examples of Latin prose, and are often read in high school Latin classes. What are they called?

*4. When did the events of this chapter occur?

CHAPTER 23

1. Name the three men of the Second Triumvirate?

2. What does triumvirate mean?

3. Where did the Triumvirate defeat Brutus and how did he die?

4. In what battle were Antony and Cleopatra defeated by Octavius, and how did they die?

5. Who was Julius Caesar's adopted son and nephew?

6. What was Octavius' name changed to and what does it mean?

*7. In what year did the Republic of Rome cease to exist and who is considered to be the first of the long line of Roman emperors?

8. What was the name of the elite military unit that guarded the Roman emperor?

9. Name some famous people who lived during the reign of Augustus?

CHAPTER 24

1. Name the four emperors of Rome after Augustus who were all tyrants.
2. How did Nero kill his stepbrother? How did he attempt to kill his mother?
3. Who did Nero blame for the burning of Rome? Who died during the subsequent persecution?
4. Name two famous authors who committed suicide upon Nero's orders.
*5. What does the expression "Nero fiddled while Rome burned" mean when applied to current politics?

CHAPTER 25

1. Following Nero, three men where made emperors by their soldiers and each ruled for a short time. Name them.
2. Who captured Jerusalem and destroyed the temple of the Jews, fulfilling the prophecy of Christ? In what year was the destruction of Jerusalem?
*3. Where in the Bible is Christ's prophecy about the destruction of Jerusalem and what does it say?
*4. What is famous about the Arch of Titus?
5. Name three building projects of Titus.
6. What two cities were destroyed by the eruption of Mt.Vesuvius during the reign of Titus?

CHAPTER 26

1. Name the two emperors after Titus.
2. Name the three areas that Trajan brought into the Empire.
3. Where was the country of Dacia and what is it called today?
4. Where was the country of Armenia and what is it called today?
5. Where was the area of Mesopotamia and what is it called today?
6. Name four building projects associated with the reign of Trajan.
7. After the reign of Trajan, what was the wish of the people of Rome about their future emperors?

CHAPTER 27

1. Name two important building projects of Hadrian that can still be seen today.
2. What was the purpose of Hadrian's wall and where was it?
*3. What became of Hadrian's tomb?
4. Why was Antonius called Pius?
5. What were the Catacombs?
6. What philosophy did Marcus Aurelius follow? What were the main beliefs of this philosophy?
7. What did Marcus Aurelius call his Christian legion and why?
*8. In what ways does Marcus Aurelius seem like a Christian?
*9. Why do you think Marcus Aurelius was not happy? What Christian virtues did he not possess?

History Questions

CHAPTER 28

1. The hundred years after the death of Marcus Aurelius are called by what name? Describe this period.
2. How were the emperors put in power during this period?
3. Who said "The Empire is too big to be ruled by one man" and divided the Empire into two parts?
4. Who was the last emperor under which there was widespread persecution of Christians?
5. Describe some of the reforms and government reorganizations of Diocletion.
*6. Why do you think most of his reforms were unsuccessful?

CHAPTER 29

1. Who was the first Roman emperor to become a Christian?
*2. Constantine saw a vision of a cross before what battle?
3. What words were written on the cross?
4. Where did Constantine move the capital of the Roman Empire to, and what did he name the city?

CHAPTER 30

1. What emperor after Constantine tried to reestablish the pagan religion of ancient Rome?
2. What did he attempt to do in order to prove the Christian religion untrue?
3. What happened when work began on the Temple? What did Julian the Apostate say as he was dying?
4. Beginning with Valentinian the empire was usually ruled by two emperors. What were they called?
5. What emperor was publicly shamed by Ambrose, the bishop of Milan?
6. Who was the last emperor of the West, who replaced him, and in what year did the Roman Empire of the West come to an end?
7. In what year did the Roman Empire of the East come to an end?

THE IMPERIAL REPUBLIC
264 B.C.- 27 B.C.

264-146 B.C.   **THE PUNIC WARS**

Regulus	1st Punic War, started in Sicily, lost an army in Africa Word of honor and Rome over self
	2nd Punic War, worst defeat in Roman history at Cannae to Hannibal
Fabius	Delaying tactics
Scipio Africanus	Defeated Hannibal at Zama
Cato the Censor	3rd Punic War, Carthage sowed with salt. *Delenda est Carthago*

146-27 B.C.   **THE REPUBLIC BREAKS DOWN**

The Gracchi	Tiberius	Agrarian bill, clubbed to death by senators in Assembly
	Caius	Accused of wanting to be king, died in mob violence
	Marius	Teutones, Cimbri, Ambrones, dictator general, exile in Carthage, vengeance on nobles.
Social War 90-87 B.C. *(war with Italian allies)*	Sulla	Fame in Social War, enemy of Marius. King Mithridates of Pontus Sulla first to bring his army into Rome. Dictator general, massacre of Marians
	Pompey the Great	Pirates, defeated Mithridates, reorganized Asia under Roman rule. Dictator general, 1st Triumvirate - Pompey, Caesar, Crassus

Civil War 49-27 B.C.

Julius Caesar	Soldier, statesman, scholar, orator Conquest of Gaul - 8 yrs., *De Bello Gallico*, invasion of Britain. Pompey declared Caesar to be an enemy of Rome. Crossed the Rubicon. Dictator of Rome. Julian calendar. Assassinated 44 B.C.
Cicero	Greatest orator. Catiline orations. Put to death by order of Mark Antony.

THE ROMAN EMPIRE
27 B.C. - 476 A.D.

PAX ROMANA
27 B.C. - 180 A.D.

Augustus *Octavius given title in 27B.C.*	Grandnephew of Caesar, adopted son. 2nd Triumvirate - Octavius, Antony, Lepidus. Defeated Brutus and Cassius at Philippi, defeated Antony and Cleopatra at Actium. End of Civil War and beginning of Pax Romana (200 years of peace and prosperity)

64 A.D. *persecution*

Tiberius
Caligula
Claudius
Nero

Jesus crucified during reign of Tiberius
The four tyrant emperors
First Roman persecution of
Christians under Nero

Galba
Otho
Vitellius

Generals put in power by army, each for only a few months.

70 A.D.

Vespasian
Titus, his son

Destruction of Jerusalem
Arch of Titus, Colosseum,
Destruction of Pompeii by
Mt. Vesuvius

Domitian

Killed flies

Nerva	
Trajan	Enlarged empire: Dacia, Armenia Mesopotamia. Trajan's Forum, Column As great as Augustus and as good as Trajan.
Hadrian	Hadrian's Wall, Tomb (Castel St. Angelo)
Antoninus Pius	good to Christians
Marcus Aurelius	Stoic, Thundering Legion, A virtuous pagan.

MILITARY ANARCHY
180- 285 A.D.

Corruption, taxes, inflation, crime
Impoverishment of middle class.

REORGANIZATION AND FALL
OF ROMAN EMPIRE

285. A.D.	Diocletian	Divided empire in two. Emperor of East and Emperor of West. Last widespread persecution of Christians.
307 A.D.	Constantine the Great	The first Christian emperor. Battle of Milvian Bridge. Moved capital from Rome to Constantinople.
363 A.D.	Julian the Apostate	Gave up Christian religion and reconverted to paganism. Tried to rebuild the Temple in Jerusalem.
380 A.D.	Theodosius	Capital of Western empire in Milan. Bishop of Milan, Ambrose, made Theodosius do penance for massacre before he could come to church.

End of Western Empire
476 A.D.	Romulus Augustulus	Last Roman emperor. Deposed by a barbarian soldier, Odoacer

End of Eastern Empire
1453 A.D.		Constantinople fell to the Turks.

Grammar Forms

VERBS

Regular principal parts

First conjugation	**voco, vocare, vocavi, vocatus**
Second conjugation	**moneo, monére, monui, monitus**
Third conjugation	**rego, regere**
Fourth conjugation	**audio, audire, audivi, auditus**

Present tense

	First conjugation		Second	Third	Fourth	*To be* Verb
S.						
1 P.	**voco**	*I call, am calling, do call*	moneo	rego	audio	sum
2 P.	**vocas**	*you call, are calling, do call*	mones	regis	audis	es
3 P.	**vocat**	*he, she it calls, is calling, does call*	monet	regit	audit	est
Pl.						
1 P.	**vocamus**	*we call, are calling, do call*	monemus	regimus	audimus	sumus
2 P.	**vocatis**	*you call, are calling, do call*	monetis	regitis	auditis	estis
3 P.	**vocant**	*they call, are calling, do call*	monent	regunt	audiunt	sunt

Imperfect tense

S.						
1 P.	**vocabam**	*I was calling*	monebam	regebam	audiebam	eram
2 P.	**vocabas**	*you were calling*	monebas	regebas	audiebas	eras
3 P.	**vocabat**	*he, she,it was calling*	monebat	regebat	audiebat	erat
Pl.						
1 P.	**vocabamus**	*we were calling*	monebamus	regebamus	audiebamus	eramus
2 P.	**vocabatis**	*you were calling*	monebatis	regebatis	audiebatis	eratis
3 P.	**vocabant**	*they were calling*	monebant	regebant	audiebant	erant

Future tense

S.						
1 P.	**vocabo**	*I will call*	monebo	-	-	ero
2 P.	**vocabis**	*you will call*	monebis			eris
3 P.	**vocabit**	*he, she, it will call*	monebit			erit
Pl.						
1 P.	**vocabimus**	*we will call*	monebimus	-	-	erimus
2 P.	**vocabitis**	*you will call*	monebitis			eritis
3 P.	**vocabunt**	*they will call*	monebunt			erunt

PRONOUNS

First Person S.		Pl.		Second Person S.		Pl.	
ego	*I*	nos	*we*	tu	*you*	vos	*you*
mei	*me*	nostri,um	*us*	tui	*you*	vestri, um	*you*
mihi	*me*	nobis	*us*	tibi	*you*	vobis	*you*
me	*me*	nos	*us*	te	*you*	vos	*you*
me	*me*	nobis	*us*	te	*you*	vobis	*you*

NOUNS

	First Declension		Second Declension			
	1st decl. F.		**2nd decl. M.**		**2nd decl. N.**	
	S.	*Pl.*	*S.*	*Pl.*	*S.*	*Pl.*
Nominative	mensa	mensae	**servus**	**servi**	donum	dona
Genitive	mensae	mensarum	**servi**	**servorum**	doni	donorum
Dative	mensae	mensis	**servo**	**servis**	dono	donis
Accusative	mensam	mensas	**servum**	**servos**	donum	dona
Ablative	mensa	mensis	**servo**	**servis**	dono	donis

3rd decl. M/F		**3rd decl. N**		**i stem**		**4th decl.**		**5th decl.**	
lex	leges	flumen	flumina	**pars**	**partes**	portus	portus	res	res
legis	legum	fluminis	fluminum	**partis**	**partium**	portus	portuum	rei	rerum
legi	legibus	flumini	fluminibus	**parti**	**partibus**	portui	portibus	rei	rebus
legem	leges	flumen	flumina	**partem**	**partes**	portum	portus	rem	res
lege	legibus	flumine	fluminibus	**parte**	**partibus**	portu	portibus	re	rebus

CASE ENDINGS

1 st decl. F.		**2nd decl. M.**		**2nd decl. N.**	
S.	*Pl.*	*S.*	*Pl.*	*S.*	*Pl.*
a	ae	us,er,ir	i	um	a
ae	arum	i	orum	i	orum
ae	is	o	is	o	is
am	as	um	os	um	a
a	is	o	is	o	is

3rd decl. M/ F.		**3rd decl. N**		**4th decl.**		**5th decl.**	
S.	*Pl.*	*S.*	*Pl.*	*S.*	*Pl.*	*S.*	*Pl.*
—	es	—	a	us	us	es	es
is	**i**um	is	um	us	uum	ei	erum
i	ibus	i	ibus	ui	ibus	ei	ebus
em	es	—	a	um	us	em	es
e	ibus	e	ibus	u	ibus	e	ebus

ADJECTIVES
First and second declension adjectives

	Masculine		*Feminine*		*Neuter*	
	S.	*Pl.*	*S.*	*Pl.*	*S.*	*Pl.*
Nominative	bonus	boni	bona	bonae	bonum	bona
Genitive	boni	bonorum	bonae	bonarum	boni	bonorum
Dative	bono	bonis	bonae	bonis	bono	bonis
Accusative	bonum	bonos	bonam	bonas	bonum	bona
Ablative	bono	bonis	bona	bonis	bono	bonis

Latin Sayings

1. Retro, Satana! — Get thee behind me, Satan!
2. Natura non facit saltum — Nature does not make leaps
3. Magister dixit — The master has spoken
4. Repetitio mater studiorum — Repetition is the mother of learning
5. Hannibal ad portas! — Hannibal at the gates!
6. Errare est humanum *(Seneca)* — To err is human
7. Caveat emptor — Let the buyer beware
8. Credo in unum Deum — I believe in one God
9. Arma virumque cano *(1st line of Aeneid)* — I sing of arms and a man
10. Ave Caesar, morituri te salutamus *(Roman gladiators)* — Hail Caesar, we who are about to die salute you
11. Hodie Christus natus est — Today Christ is born
12. Non oratorem, non senatorem, sed piscatorem. *(St. Augustine)* — Not an orator, not a senator, but a fisherman.
13. Delenda est Carthago *(Cato the elder)* — Carthage must be destroyed
14. Romanus civis sum — I am a citizen of Rome
15. O tempora, O mores *(Cicero)* — O the times, O the customs
16. Etiam capillus unus habet umbram *(Publius Syrus)* — Even one hair has a shadow
17. O, praeclarum custodem ovium lupum. *(Cicero)* — O, excellent protector of sheep, the wolf.
18. Dies Irae — Day of wrath
19. Deo gratias — Thanks be to God

ab,a, *prep. w. abl.*	from, away from
acies, aciei, *f.*	battle line
ad, *prep. w. acc.*	to, toward, near
adoro, (1)	adore
adventus, us, *m.*	arrival, coming
aeternus, a, um	eternal, everlasting
ager, agri, *m.*	field (agricultural)
agnus, i, *m.*	lamb
ago, agere	do, drive, act, treat
agricola, ae, *m.*	farmer
albus, a, um	white
alienus, a, um	foreign, unfavorable
almus, a, um	nurturing, kindly
altus, a, um	high, deep
ambulo, (1)	walk
amicus, i , *m.*	friend
amo, (1)	love
angelus, i, *m.*	angel
animus, i., *m.*	mind, spirit
annus, i, *m.*	year
ante, *prep. w. acc.*	before
aperio, aperire	open
apostolus, i, *m.*	apostle
appello, (1)	speak to, address
aqua, ae, *f.*	water
aquarius	water carrier
aquila, ae, *f.*	eagle
ara, ae, *f.*	altar
arbor, arboris, *f.*	tree
aries	ram
aro, (1)	plow
ars, artis, *f.*	art, skill
audio, (4)	hear
augeo, augére	increase
auriga, ae, *c.*	charioteer
aurora, ae, *f.*	dawn
autem	however
auxilium, i. *n.*	help, aid
avis, avis, *f.*	bird
barbarus, i. *n.*	barbarian
beatus, a, um	blessed
bellum, i, *n.*	war
bene	well
bibo, bibere	drink
bonus, a, um	good
cado, cadere	fall
caelum, i *n.*	heaven
Caesar, Caesaris, *m.*	Caesar
campus, i *m.*	field (athletic, assembly)
cancer	crab
canis, canis, *c.*	dog
cano, canere	sing
capillus, i *m.*	hair
capricorn	goat
caput, capitis, *n.*	head
caritas, caritatis, *f.*	love, charity
carmen, carminis, *n.*	song

Latin-English Vocabulary

casa, ae, *f.*	cottage
caveo, cavére	guard against, beware of
cena, ae, *f.*	dinner
centurio, centurionis, *m.*	centurion
certus, a, um	certain, sure
Christianus, a, um	Christian
Christianus, i	a Christian
Christus, i. *m.*	Christ
cibus, i. *m.*	food
circum, *prep. w. acc.*	around, about
cithara, ae, *f.*	harp
civis, civis, *c.*	citizen
civitas, civitatis, *f.*	state
clam, *adv.*	secretly
clamo, (1)	shout
clamor, clamoris, *m.*	shout, shouting
clarus, a, um	clear, bright, famous
claudo, claudere	shut
collis, collis, *m.*	hill
contra, *prep. w. acc.*	against
cor, cordis, *n.*	heart
corona, ae, *f.*	crown
corpus, corporis, *n.*	body
cras, *adv.*	tomorrow
credo, credere	believe
crux, crucis, *f.*	cross
culina, ae, *f.*	kitchen
culpa, ae, *f.*	fault, crime
cum, *prep. w. abl.*	with
cupidus, a, um	eager, desirous
cur	why
curro, currere	run
custos, custodis, *m.*	guard
de, *prep. w. abl.*	down from
debeo, (2)	owe, ought
debitum, i. *n.*	debt, trespass
defendo, defendere	defend
dens, dentis, *m.*	tooth
Deus, i *m.*	God
dico, dicere	say, tell
dies, diei, *m.*	day
discipulus, i *m.*	student
diu, *adv.*	for a long time
do, dare, dedi, datus	give
doceo, docére	teach
dolor, doloris, *m.*	pain, sorrow
dominus, i *m.*	lord, master
donum, i, *n.*	gift
dormio, (4)	sleep
duco, ducere, duxi, ductus	lead, guide
dux, ducis, *m.*	leader
ecclesia, ae, *f.*	church
edo, edere	eat
ego, mei	I, me
epistula, ae, *f.*	letter
equitatus, us, *m.*	cavalry
equus, i *m.*	horse

erro, (1)	err
et	and
etiam	also
Evangelium, i, *n.*	gospel
ex, *prep. w. abl.*	out of
exercitus, us, *m.*	army
exspecto, (1)	wait for
fabula, ae, *f.*	story
facies, faciei, *f.*	face
fama, ae, *f.*	fame, rumor, report
femina, ae, *f.*	woman
fenestra, ae, *f.*	window
fides, fidei, *f.*	faith, loyalty
filia, ae, *f.*	daughter
filius, i *m.*	son
finio (4)	finish
finis, finis, *m.*	end, boundary
fleo, flére	cry, weep
flumen, fluminis, *n.*	river
fons, fontis, *m.*	fountain
fortuna, ae, *f.*	fortune, chance
forum, i, *n.*	forum
frater, fratris, *m.*	brother
fructus, us, *m.*	fruit, profit, enjoyment
frumentum, i, *n.*	grain, crops
fuga, ae, *f.*	flight
Gallia, ae, *f.*	Gaul
Gallus, i, *m.*	a Gaul
gaudium, i *n.*	joy
geminus, i. *m.*	twin
gens, gentis, *f.*	tribe
gladius, i, *m.*	sword
gloria, ae, *f.*	glory, fame
gratia, ae, *f.*	grace, thanks
habeo, (2)	have
habito, (1)	live, inhabit, dwell
herba, ae, *f.*	herb, plant
heri, *adv.*	yesterday
Hispania, ae, *f.*	Spain
hodie	today
homo, hominis, *m.*	man
hora, ae, *f.*	hour
hortus, i, *m.*	garden
hostis, hostis, *c.*	enemy
ignis, ignis. *f.*	fire
impedio, (4)	hinder
imperator, imperatoris, *m.*	general, commander
imperium, i, *n.*	command, empire
impetus, us, *m.*	attack
in, *prep. w. acc. or abl.*	in, on, into, against
injuria, ae, *f.*	injury
insula, ae, *f.*	island
inter, *prep. w. acc.*	between, among
ira, ae, *f.*	anger
Italia, ae, *f.*	Italy
itaque	therefore
iter, itineris, *n.*	journey, march, route

janua, ae, *f.*	door
Jesus, Jesu	Jesus
jubeo, jubére	order, command
judico, (1)	judge
jus, juris, *n.*	right
laboro, (1)	work
lacus, us, *m.*	lake
laetus, a, um	happy
laudo, (1)	praise
lavo, (1)	wash
lectio, lectionis, *f.*	lesson
legatus, i, *m.*	lieutenant, envoy
legio, legionis, *f.*	legion
leo	lion
lex, legis, *f.*	law
liber, libri, *m.*	book
libero, (1)	set free
libertas, libertatis, *f.*	freedom, liberty
libra	pair of scales
lingua, ae, *f.*	language, tongue
locus, i *m.*	place
longus, a um	long
Lucia, ae, *f.*	Lucy
luna, ae, *f.*	moon
lupus, i, *m.*	wolf
lux, lucis, *f.*	light
magister, magistri, *m.*	teacher, master
magnus, a, um	large, great
malus, a, um	bad
mandatum, i, *n.*	commandment
maneo, manére	remain, stay
Marcus, i	Mark
mare, maris, *n.*	sea
Maria, ae, *f.*	Mary
mater, matris, *f.*	mother
memoria, ae, *f.*	memory
mens, mentis, *f.*	mind
mensa, ae, *f.*	table
meridies, ei, *m.*	midday, noon
meus, a, um	my
miles, militis, *m.*	soldier
mitto, mittere, misi, missus	send
moneo (2)	warn
mons, montis, *m.*	mountain
mora, ae, *f.*	delay
mors, mortis, *f.*	death
mos, moris *m.*	custom
moveo, movére	move
multus, a, um	much, many
mundus, i, *m.*	world
munio, (4)	fortify, construct
murus, i, *m.*	wall
narro, (1)	tell
nato, (1)	swim
natura, ae, *f.*	nature
nauta, ae, *m.*	sailor
navigo, (1)	sail

navis, navis, *f.*	ship
nihil	nothing
nimbus, i, *m.*	cloud
nix, nivis, *f.*	snow
nomen, nominis, *n.*	name
non	not
nos, nostri, *(personal pronoun)*	we, us
novus, a, um	new
nox, noctis, *f.*	night
numquam, *adv.*	never
nunc	now
nuntius, i, *m.*	message, messenger
occupo, (1)	seize
oculus, i, *m.*	eye
oppidum, I, *n.*	town
opus, operis, *n.*	work, deed
orator, oratoris, *m.*	speaker, orator
orbis, orbis, *m.*	world, orbit, circle
ordo, ordinis, *m.*	order, rank
oro, (1)	pray, speak
os, oris, *n.*	mouth
ovis, ovis, *f.*	sheep
panis, panis, *m.*	bread
paro, (1)	prepare
pars, partis, *f.*	part
parvus, a, um	small
passio, passionis, *f.*	suffering
pastor, pastoris, *m.*	shepherd
pater, patris, *m.*	father
patria, ae, *f.*	fatherland, country
pax, pacis, *f.*	peace
peccatum, i, *n.*	sin, mistake
pecunia, ae, *f.*	money
per, *prep. w. acc.*	through
periculum, i, *n.*	danger, peril
pes, pedis, *m.*	foot
peto, petere	seek, beg
piscator, piscatoris, *m.*	fisherman
pisces	fish
placeo, placére	please
plenus, a, um	full
poeta, ae, *m.*	poet
pono, ponere, posui, positus	put, place, set
pons, pontis, *m.*	bridge
populus, i, *m.*	people
porta, ae, *f.*	gate, door
porto, (1)	carry
portus, us, *m.*	harbor
post, *prep. w. acc.*	after, behind
praemium, i *n.*	reward
primus, a, um	first
principium, i, *n.*	beginning, foundation
proelium, i, *n.*	battle
prohibeo, (2)	prevent
provincia, ae, *f.*	province
proximus, a, um	next, nearest
puella, ae, *f.*	girl

puer, pueri, *m.*	boy
pugna, ae, *f.*	fight
pugno, (1)	fight
punio, (4)	punish
quid	what
quis	who
regina, ae, *f.*	queen
regnum, i, *n.*	kingdom
rego, regere	rule
res, rei, *f.*	thing
respondeo, respondére	respond, answer
rex, regis, *m.*	king
rideo, ridére	laugh
Roma, ae, *f.*	Rome
Romanus, a, um	Roman
Romanus, i, m.	a Roman
rus, ruris, *n.*	countryside
saeculum, i *n.*	time, period, age, world
saepe	often
sagittarius	archer
sal, salis, *n.*	salt, sea water
saluto, (1)	greet
sanctus, a, um	holy, saint
scientia, ae, *f.*	knowledge
scio, (4)	know
scorpio	scorpion
scribo, scribere	write
scutum, i, *n.*	shield
secundus, a, um	second
sed	but
sedeo, sedére	sit
sedes, sedis, *f.*	seat, abode
sella, ae, *f.*	chair
semper	always
senator, senatoris, *m.*	senator
senatus, us, *m.*	senate
sentio, sentire	feel, perceive, think
servo, (1)	guard, keep
servus, i, *m.*	slave, servant
sicut	as
signum, i, *n.*	sign, standard
silva, ae, *f.*	forest
sine, *prep. w. abl.*	without
socius, i, *m.*	ally
sol, solis, *m.*	sun
solus, a, um	alone, only
soror, sororis, *f.*	sister
specto, (1)	look at
spes, spei, *f.*	hope
spiritus, us, *m.*	spirit
statim	immediately
stella , ae, *f.*	star
sto, stare, steti, status	stand
studium, i, *n.*	enthusiasm, zeal, learning
sub, *prep. w. acc. or abl.*	under, at foot of
summus, a, um	highest
supero, (1)	overcome, conquer

supra, *prep. w. acc.*	over, above
tabella, ae, *f.*	tablet
taberna, ae, *f.*	shop
taurus, i, *m.*	bull
telum, i, *n.*	weapon, dart
tempto, (1)	tempt
tempus, temporis, *n.*	time
teneo, tenére	hold
tentatio, tentationis, *f.*	temptation
tergum, i. *n.*	back
terra, ae, *f.*	land, earth
terreo, (2)	frighten, terrify
tertius, a, um	third
timeo, timére	fear
timor, timoris, *m.*	fear
toga, ae, *f.*	toga
tollo, tollere	take away, raise up
totus, a, um	whole
trado, tradere	hand over, deliver up
trans, *prep. w. acc.*	across
tu, tui, *personal pronoun, sing.*	you
tuba, ae, *f.*	trumpet
tum	then
tutus, a, um	safe
tuus, a, um	your (one person)
ubi	where
umbra,ae, *f.*	shadow
unda, ae, *f.*	wave
undique	from all sides
urbs, urbis, *f.*	city
ursa, ae, *f.*	bear
usus, us, *m.*	use, experience
valeo, valére	am well, am strong
vallum, i *n.*	wall, rampart
venio, venire	come
ventus, i, *m.*	wind
ver, veris, *n.*	spring
verbum, i, *n.*	word
veritas, veritatis , *f.*	truth
verus, a, um	true
via, ae, *f.*	road, way
victoria, ae, *f.*	victory
vicus, i , *m.*	town, village
video, vidére	see
villa, ae, *f.*	farmhouse
vinco, vincere, vici, victus	conquer
vinum, i, *n.*	wine
vir, viri, *m.*	man
virgo, virginis, *f.*	virgin
virtus, virtutis, *f.*	virtue, courage
vita, ae, *f.*	life
vivo, vivere	live
voco, (1)	call
voluntas, voluntatis, *f.*	will, good will
vos, vestri, *personal pronoun, plural*	you
vox, vocis, *f.*	voice
vulnus, vulneris, *n.*	wound

LATINA CHRISTIANA II FLASH-CARDS

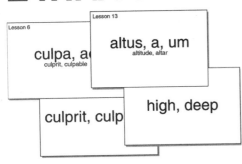

Flashcards for *Latina Christiana I & II* contain all of the vocabulary, cue words, conjugations, and declensions from their respective *Latina Christiana* courses. Each word is also color coded by part of speech (i.e. nouns and pronouns are blue, verbs are green, adjectives are Red, etc.), and they are specially sized for younger hands. Save yourself some time and frustration with these wonderful flashcards.

LATINA CHRISTIANA II DVDs

Latina Christiana DVDs are taught by Leigh Lowe, author of Prima Latina and a teacher at Highlands Latin School. Mrs. Lowe's engaging personality and experience in front of young students provide a comfortable and inviting environment for introductory Latin study.

Order *Latina Christiana Flash-cards and DVDs* from your favorite book seller or www.MemoriaPress.com

ABOUT THE AUTHOR

Cheryl Lowe became interested in Latin and classical education while homeschooling her sons 15 years ago. After studying and teaching for several years, Cheryl wrote her first Latin book, *Latina Christiana*, an introductory Latin course for parents with no Latin background. Because of her own experience learning and teaching Latin, *Latina Christiana* has been critically judged by nearly every reviewer as the best Latin program available for parents or teachers with little Latin background. Since its first publication, Latina Christiana has been adopted by hundreds of school and used by nearly 50,000 homeschoolers to learn Latin.

For the last 10 years, Cheryl has been teaching *Latina Christiana* and improving her line of thoughtfully prepared Latin courses which now include *Latina Christiana, Lingua Angelica,* and a soon to be released comprehensive program called *First Form Latin.* Cheryl also directs the vision for all of the Memoria Press courses.

Cheryl started Memoria Press to serve parents and schools who seek excellence in education by developing and publishing classical education material. Unlike many textbook publishers that "write by committee", Memoria Press is unique because all of its courses are developed in the classroom at Highlands Latin School, the cottage school Cheryl created to implement her vision of classical education. Because Memoria Press' courses have been written and rewritten by real teachers in a classical, cottage school, Memoria Press has gained a reputation for producing outstanding courses that work at home or in the classroom.

Cheryl's teaching experience includes college, high school, homeschool, and cottage school. She has taught hundreds of homeschooled and classroom students and feels that her greatest teaching accomplishment is that her students master Latin grammar before high school. Cheryl's education includes a B.A. in Chemistry and a M.S. in Biology. She is also a certified teacher in chemistry, biology, math, and history.